Peace Comes
Dropping Slow

Denis Bradley was born in Buncrana, County Donegal, but has spent most of his adult life in Derry city. He is a former priest, who has also worked as a counsellor and set up shelters for the homeless and treatment centres for alcohol and drug addiction. He was the first vice chair of the Northern Ireland Policing Board, set up to oversee the actions of the Police Service of Northern Ireland, and as a member of the so-called 'backchannel', who acted as go-betweens for the IRA and the British government, was instrumental in helping bring about the Good Friday Agreement.

Peace Comes Dropping Slow

My Life in the Troubles

Denis Bradley

MERRION
PRESS

First published in 2024 by
Merrion Press
10 George's Street
Newbridge
Co. Kildare
Ireland
www.merrionpress.ie

978 1 78537 500 2 (Paper)
978 1 78537 501 9 (Ebook)

A CIP catalogue record for this book is
available from the British Library.

Typeset in Sabon LT Std 11.5/17 pt

Cover design by riverdesignbooks.com
Front cover image courtesy of Margaret McLaughlin

Merrion Press is a member of Publishing Ireland.

CONTENTS

PROLOGUE

McGUINNESS HIMSELF OPENED THE DOOR. That was a relief. Better to have him on his own for a few minutes than have to ask his mother if Martin was in the house. I was worried that Gerry Kelly might have already gone back to Belfast, as it must have been at least half an hour since Noel Gallagher had delivered the message that they were not going ahead with the meeting because only one person from the British government side had turned up.

McGuinness would find it harder to refuse me face to face. But to be honest, I was also glad it was him because I was a little unsure of his mother, Peggy, on whose front door I had just knocked. We got on very well, but there was an edge to her that made me wary. I had seen that edge – a burst of deep anger – on a few occasions and it was something that left an impression. McGuinness had it too. He had inherited some of Peggy's temperament.

When McGuinness opened his mother's front door that night in March 1993, and before he could say anything, I told him that Robert McLarnon, more frequently referred to by his MI5 code name Fred, was in my car, which was parked farther up the street. I was amazed that Fred had agreed to go with me into the heart of the Bogside where he could have been abducted and used for ransom. I said to McGuinness that he and Gerry Kelly should talk to Fred, that they should give him a chance to explain why he had come on his own, even though the original agreement had been that two British government officials would meet with two representatives of the Provos.

McGuinness didn't say anything but gave me one of those looks that inferred, *You are chancing your arm again, Bradley.* That was enough for me to go to the car and tell Fred that we were going into the house. When we entered, Gerry Kelly and Peggy were in the living room watching television. Kelly and I had never met, so he would have seen two strange men following Martin into the house. He would later berate me for bringing a British agent to McGuinness' mother's home.

As Fred and I entered the house, McGuinness nodded at Kelly and both men moved into the kitchen, followed by myself and Fred. I closed the kitchen door and made the introductions. I knew I had only a few minutes to make the pitch and to try to change the atmosphere. I acknowledged that the agreement had been for two people from the British side to attend and said I would leave Fred to explain why he was on his own. I also pointed out that a mountain of work had been done on both sides and it would be wrong to get hung up on a formality. It would be best if the three of them talked together without me. I was going to go and chat to Peggy, giving them the opportunity to talk together and decide what to do. For everybody's sake, I said, it was important that the meeting take place. Then I left.

I knew that if this meeting didn't go ahead, then it could be the end – the end of almost twenty years of hard work to make it to this point, the end of potential talks between the British government and republicans. The result would not be good for Ireland.

Twenty minutes later McGuinness opened the kitchen door and nodded to me. The meeting was back on.

1

Beginnings

I AM ONE OF THOSE northerners who wasn't born in the North. The town of Buncrana, ten miles from the Irish border and twelve from Derry city, is where I was born. It lies on the Inishowen peninsula, which sits at the most northern part of Donegal, beside County Derry, one of the six northern counties that was hived off from the rest of Ireland in the settlement that brought partition to the island of Ireland and created Northern Ireland. Inishowen is physically attached to Donegal as well as to Derry, and emotionally attached to both.

My parents were reared in a townland called the Illies, six miles or so outside the town. The name is probably derived from the Irish word for elbow, although I never could see that connection in the landscape. A mile off the main road to the Illies is an even smaller townland consisting of four houses called the Big Hill, the birthplace of my father, and at the bottom of that same hill is where my mother was born. As was the custom, the homestead on the Big Hill, a few rush-filled fields and bogland of four or five turf banks, was left to the eldest son, in this case Ownie, or 'Big Ownie' as we always called him. But my father wasn't completely left out of the inheritance. He was left the turbary rights to two of the turf banks at the edge of the small farm. Our family cut turf there every summer.

My mother ran a guest house in Buncrana, which was busy during the spring and summer months, and when all the beds in the house and a few in an outhouse were occupied, one or other of us young ones was sent up to the Big Hill. Those were the years when a boat sailed out of Glasgow three nights a week during the summer months and arrived in Derry the next morning. My father drove one of the buses for the Londonderry and Lough Swilly Railway Co. that met the Glasgow boat at five o'clock in the morning and dispersed its passengers throughout the small towns and villages of Donegal.

My mother was an only child. Her father died when she was a baby and her mother emigrated to America, leaving her with an aunt, who lived with us. We called her Ba. I presume the name arose because the young ones couldn't say Bridget. My grandmother did not keep in touch with her sister or her child, and any knowledge of her whereabouts and her life only surfaced after the Second World War, when a local solicitor delivered a box that had come from the American Army with my mother's name attached. It was from a half-brother she didn't know existed, who had named her his next of kin, and the parcel contained a few personal items, such as a small crucifix, which I still have. He had been killed in action somewhere in France towards the end of the war.

That history left an edge on my mother's personality. She was determined and overly respectful of respectability. She was hard-working, capable and ambitious for her children. Her story of parental emigration and of being reared by an in-law was a common one in Ireland, but the complete surprise of discovering and losing a sibling in the same moment is remarkable enough. The hurt she felt and seldom spoke of was greatly tempered by the respect and love my father poured on her. That softened her for the greater part and the respectability imbalance only became dominant when any of my brothers or sisters broke the moral standards of the time and when I chose to leave the priesthood. She found my leaving and getting married very difficult to come to terms with and fluctuated from sorrow to anger and back again. She wasn't alone in that reaction, but slowly, over the years, she mellowed and grew very fond of, and even close to, my wife, Mary, and my three children.

But if my mother's familial history was constrained and traumatic, my father's family was normal and typical – four females and three males born into a small house on the side of a mountain, which officially was called Meenamullaghan but was known to everyone as the Big Hill. During my childhood, Aunts Fanny and Kitty and their families lived in the two-bedroom, low-strung house attached to a byre where two cows had their beds, and a few hens and geese had their nests. A couple of days on the Big Hill was enjoyable, but too long and I became homesick. I didn't like the smell of the blankets on the bed, and I was a bit afraid of Granny Bradley, who occupied a 'settled' bed in the corner of the kitchen. I never saw her out of that bed because she had a breathing problem. She scolded a lot, and I never forgave her for making Aunt Fanny put butter in my egg because I had complained that it was too hard.

My father was a quiet, gentle man. I only remember him losing his temper with me on one occasion and because it was so unusual and unexpected, I still remember him skelping me around the legs. I think he gifted me the softer parts of my nature and also an understanding that softer did not necessarily equate with weaker. He had his standards and convictions and the strength and determination to stick with them. He was also an avid listener to radio news, often leaving one channel to tune into a further bulletin elsewhere, an annoying habit that I now find myself doing more often than I should.

Not a 'pub' man, it would have been a very infrequent occasion that my father would have spent time in any of the public houses in the town – something of which there was no shortage. I once counted them and there were more than twenty on the main street alone. Many of the fathers of the children I played with on the streets would have gone to the pub most evenings. When, during the early years of my priesthood, I got involved in setting up a hostel for street-drinking men and a treatment facility for people suffering with drug and alcohol addiction, I was often asked about the reason for my involvement. It was sometimes insinuated that I had personal or familial experience and I had, but not in the way people thought.

Being a well-built young man with broad shoulders, my father was often called upon to go out into the bog and carry men home over his shoulders to their wives and children. He described scenes of very drunk men huddled around, drinking poitín as it dripped out of the still. Men who were past caring and who lived only for the next drink. It wasn't as bad as that in my childhood, but I was aware of many fathers staggering home of an evening, worse for wear from the drink.

While my father did take an occasional drink, I don't ever remember a time when he drank to excess. Although he never joined a political party, it is perhaps telling that the strongest political opinion my father had was his support for the nascent Irish government in its battle against the making and distribution of poitín. In this it was backed by the Catholic Church, and for a time, in the adolescent years of the Irish State, the Church made this a reserved sin. That meant that an ordinary parish priest or curate could not grant forgiveness for such activities. It was reserved to the bishop of the diocese to perform that function. There are plenty of stories of queues of men outside the bishop's house and the banter that took place between the seekers of forgiveness. So, while I didn't consciously get involved in helping those with alcohol and drug problems because of my father, probably subconsciously some of his awareness and empathy for the problem seeped into me.

I was the youngest of a family of seven, eight if you include Frances, who died in childhood. There are advantages and disadvantages to being the youngest. I was often told that I was spoiled, and I wouldn't deny that I felt very protected and 'seen to' by my parents, four sisters and two brothers. But many of the unfulfilled ambitions of my parents for their children cascaded down through the others and landed in my lap, especially in relation to education. There were few enough children in the neighbourhood who went on to secondary education and even fewer to third level. My parents had sent my oldest brother to college for a few years and my oldest sister to a secretarial academy, but both had dropped out by the time I was leaving primary school.

I was no genius, but I was always on the academically capable side, mostly well behaved and much too timid not to have my homework done. So, I was destined to stay at school. I ended up as a boarder in St Columb's College in Derry. It was big and cold and the food so bad that I was hungry for the greater part of five years. There was an underlying homesickness, but I was not always unhappy there. I made good friends, and it enabled me to grow a resilience that I think helped me in later life.

Nobody was overly surprised when, at the end of those five years, I applied to go to Maynooth College to study for the priesthood. Our family home was only a stone's throw from the local church and when I had reached the requisite age I became an altar boy. The decision to enter the priesthood was not really a conscious decision but came about more by a process of elimination – visualising other roles and professions and rejecting them. There were no moments of blinding insight or divine intervention, but there was a deep attraction to the role that was strong and persistent.

September 1964 was to be the start date for my first term in Maynooth Seminary, but a few weeks before that I was told in a phone call that the bishop had decided to send me and another student to the Irish College in Rome, to undertake our clerical training and study there rather than in Maynooth. My family was delighted, and the neighbours were impressed. Those were the days when a priest in the family was a badge of honour, and one trained in Rome had an added prestige. Tellingly, I was much more excited by the fact that I would still be able to go to the Derry City football match against Steaua Bucureşti in the European Cup Winners' Cup in September because I would not have to go to Rome until October.

I soon discovered that the reason I was being sent to Rome was to save the bishop money. Because the other student and I were from Donegal, we were not eligible for a financial grant for third-level education, so it was cheaper for the bishop to send us rather than two students from the north of Ireland. But whatever the reason, I gained much from studying in Rome. The college was small – sixty or so students, who had to fully enter social, sporting and organisational engagement, way beyond what would be necessary and demanded in a larger institution. I was not good at any of those activities, but because of the small numbers I had no choice but to debate and act and play games within the college and against other colleges. These were things I would never have done or been good enough to do in St Columb's College, and certainly not had I been sent to Maynooth, where hundreds of young men were trained for the priesthood at any one time. Small was beautiful for a shy young fellow, although I felt like I was going to die of homesickness in my first two weeks there.

The settling in, the entering in, was made easier because during the first two years of my time there the Second Vatican Council was in session. For part of those two years the Irish bishops lived in the college, cheek by jowl with the students, which resulted in the small college staff of three being more preoccupied with the hierarchy than with the students. The rector and his assistant, whose job it was to run the college, withdrew largely from their normal role of supervising and instructing the students in order to attend to the needs of the bishops.

The resulting free-floating, semi-independent structure of the college during those years would normally be frowned upon, but I think it was good for me. The small coterie of students had to be resilient and inventive. To an outsider it would have looked chaotic and undisciplined, and often it was, but the lack of oversight and structure encouraged and perhaps even forced me through my suffocating shyness.

I certainly wasn't overly studious. Most of the university

lectures were in Italian or, sometimes, Latin. My parents had sent me to violin lessons when I was young, and I had continued to study and play the violin through college. Technically I was reasonably good and overcame the screeching bit relatively fast, but I have always said that I have no musical ear, so I was restricted, limited in my musical ability, and that also applied to my linguistic accomplishments. Music and languages were not to be my forte.

The study was made up of two years of philosophy and four years of theology, but I spent as much time in coffee shops as I spent in the lecture halls. Whatever theology I learned was in the library, reading theologians such as James Mackey, an Irishman who was producing a lot of books at the time and gaining an international reputation. He and I would become close friends later in life. I invited him to do some consultative work when I was vice chair of the Policing Board, and I asked that he be one of the members when I was appointed co-chair of the Consultative Group on the Past.

But my main interest was reading books and articles to do with social activism. I was especially attracted to what was happening in America. Probably because I had access to American publications, the people who stood out for me were Dorothy Day, Cesar Chavez, Saul Alinsky and the Berrigan brothers, Daniel and Philip. The Berrigans, Day and Chavez were Catholics, while Alinsky had a Jewish background but worked closely with many priests in Chicago. They and their stories were the ones that stuck with me and, in retrospect, I can perceive the influence they had on my own life. Their lives and work were what initially attracted me, but the discovery that they had all been influenced by Catholic social teaching made their actions even more seductive to a young seminarian who wished for his priesthood and his Church to be socially and not just spiritually inspiring. I would have argued then and would argue still that spirituality without a strong social conscience is a conundrum and maybe a contradiction.

These five very different people had responded to different social and political needs in three very different parts of America and, in the Berrigans' case, to the war in Vietnam. Chavez, of Mexican origin, was a labour leader and community organiser in California, who worked amongst and then organised the grape and vegetable workers into trade unions. The slogan so effectively used by Barack Obama, 'Yes we can', was first used by an organisation set up by Chavez. Day was a radical journalist who established the Catholic Worker Movement to provide aid and support to the poor and homeless. She often practised civil disobedience, which on several occasions resulted in imprisonment, even in her seventies. Alinsky, for me the most interesting and influential, was born to Russian–Jewish immigrant parents and became a community activist and political theorist. Most likely agnostic, he worked closely and fruitfully with clergy from all Churches, but most especially with Catholic priests. He practised the arts of confrontation and compromise in community organising and had an unbending belief that the local community was the primary instrument of change. The Berrigans were priests – Daniel was a Jesuit who stayed in the order all his life; Philip left his order and married a former nun. Both engaged in public protests and agitation against American involvement in the Vietnam war. Daniel was the only one of them I ever met in person, when I had a cup of coffee with him in Trinity College Dublin after he delivered a lecture.

When I arrived back in Derry from Rome in 1970, the civil rights movement had been the dominant issue in politics, and on the streets Martin Luther King was the name and the inspiration known to all and sundry, especially in the Catholic, nationalist community. I was surprised, however, that none of the American activists I respected appeared to be known or spoken of among the leadership of the movement.

A few years after I arrived home, I attended a Catholic Social Action Conference in Waterford addressed by John Hume, who had included some of the better-known phrases from King in his speeches and rallying cries. I gave him a lift back to Dublin and talked to him about the American social activists that I had read about while in Rome, and, again, was greatly surprised that he was not familiar with any of them. Hume was fast becoming known on the national and international scene, but his initial activism was in helping establish the Derry Credit Union, one of the most beneficial and lasting social movements of the time. I was aware, from reading about the life of Saul Alinsky, of the criticism levelled at his prioritising of 'the local' above the national. The accusation was that this philosophy resulted in local ghettos becoming slightly better ghettos. Just months later, Hume and I would clash over the setting up of a very local organisation in the Bogside.

2

A New Parish

I WAS WORRIED WHEN I arrived back from Rome in that summer of 1970 that my first clerical appointment might be to some rural parish, far from the action that was happening on the streets of Derry and elsewhere. It was a relief when I got a phone call telling me that I was going to help in the cathedral parish in Derry for the summer months. The cathedral was situated right at the heart of what was happening on the streets of Derry, and I was very happy to be given a summer placement there.

In the few months that I was there, I learned much. I had much to learn. The hierarchical Church that had been dominant for centuries was facing a change in the attitudes and the actions of many of its parishioners. The people had taken to the streets in response to the civil rights movement. Its leaders were mainly practising Catholics, with a smattering of Protestants and Marxists, as well as an Irish republican who had been active in the IRA in the 1950s. The loudest cry was for rights and equal citizenship, but bubbling underneath was the more muffled cry for Irish unity. These were issues with which the local Catholic

Church had empathy, but it was frightened by the volume and insistency of the growing cries.

There was an instinctive knowledge that the Church was in a bind, sympathetic to the issues, yet frightened that popular action might lead to disruption and violence. There may also have been a knowledge that the influence and power of the Church itself was in question. However, I wouldn't have understood the extent and depth of the defensiveness or the threat that many of the clergy and the loyal Catholic laity felt at the time. I thought that most people would be excited and energised by the suggestions for change, within the Church itself and consequentially within Irish society, that had been stirred up by the Second Vatican Council.

I had observed some of the Council and the theological debates that accompanied it during my years in Rome. As a student I had no direct involvement with the Council, but the Irish bishops were sleeping and eating amongst us lowly students. In hindsight it is regrettable but indicative that none of the bishops or their advisers formally discussed the issues and the debates that were arising at the Council with the students. But we were all living within the ambit of the Council, and it was impossible to prevent its tentacles from spreading. I can recall the excitement of the student body when the bishops gathered in one of the college's largest rooms to come to the decision to abolish abstinence from meat on a Friday. The meeting lasted hours and word leaked out that the decision was being heavily influenced by the fear that the Irish fishing industry would be destroyed by such a decision. Economics and spirituality often go hand in hand.

I had assumed that I would be returning to a Church wrestling with the issues that had dominated that Council, coupled with the ones that had led to the unrest being demonstrated on the streets of the North. I thought that one would have fed the other – the events on the streets informing and influencing the debates and changes identified in the Council, and the vision of the Council addressing and even influencing the issues being enacted on the streets. But such is the naivety of youth.

I was now observing some of the suggested changes of the Council in situ while living in the midst of a political revolution. The Bishop of Derry, Neil Farren, was ageing and naturally uncomfortable with what was happening in the Church but even more uncomfortable with what was happening on the streets. His reputation was that of a man who had had dictatorial control over his clerics and the laity alike over a long number of years. I had got to know him slightly during his attendance at the Council and it was clear that he was increasingly discommoded by the changing times that he was being forced to face.

It was also easy to pick up divisions among the priests, most of whom were of the mind that the Church should have little engagement with what was happening on the streets, apart from the duty of speaking out against the growing violence and praying that matters would settle down and peace would return. As far as I could see, only a minority of priests thought that the Church should engage with the events on the streets and the issues that had energised those events. That minority was stymied by the hierarchical nature of the Church – not just the demarcation of stature and power, but the even more destructive clerical culture of suspicion and aversion to discussion and debate. It appeared that the majority thought that theological debate and political engagement were inappropriate for parish clergy and if the Church had anything to say or contribute, it was the responsibility and prerogative of the bishop, or even the Pope. That culture was often accompanied by cynical and cutting remarks made by many towards their fellow, more engaged priests. Indeed, there were some clerics who were famous for the quality of their put-downs. It was impossible not to admire the cleverness, the quick-wittedness and the insightfulness of their humour, while recognising the destructiveness of their gift. It took great self-assurance to ignore or get beyond certain remarks.

Perhaps surprisingly, among the two kinds of priests shaped by the Troubles – those who engaged with what was happening on the streets and those who stayed back from it as much as possible – it was not simply an age thing. In fact, some of the most active 'street priests' had been ordained years before the Troubles began. The older priests were often the most effective on the streets and the most influential with those who were thinking of joining or had already joined the IRA, because they knew their names and had known their mothers and fathers before them. It also came down to each priest's temperament, while different understandings of what priesthood meant was also a factor. Some priests felt awkward and, in their view, theology and spirituality were out of place on the streets. They felt engagement of this kind was not a role clergy should play; rather it was for the politicians and those euphemistically called 'community workers' to engage with such politics. However, others saw it as their pastoral duty to be where their parishioners were, especially where there was unrest and danger.

I understood these positions and had sympathy for both. It was not the diversity of views that frustrated me – what angered me was the failure to talk. No debate, no discussion ever took place. What impact were the Troubles having on the clergy themselves, never mind their parishioners? Men who now lived amid the chaos and the changes that were happening all around them. A discussion about how to respond, to intervene or to explore solutions might have been seen by some as too political, but it still would have been good and proper to have had those discussions. It was more than frustrating that there was no effort made to provide opportunities for these, mostly good, men to talk about what effects the Troubles were having on them personally. I became fond of saying that I came back from Rome expecting to be embroiled in a difficult and sustained discussion about these matters and that, after thirty years or more, I am still waiting for that debate.

I was still idealistic enough in those days to think that such talk was important and possible, but it was not all that many years before I despaired of priests ever being open and honest and trusting enough of each other to engage in that way. In recent years there have been many references to clericalism and the negative effect it has had on the Church. The closed, self-absorbed and cautious culture that thrived and hardened amongst a male-only priesthood had as damaging an effect on the priests themselves as it had on the institution.

Even when Eddie Daly, a confirmed 'street priest', became bishop, those conversations didn't take place. Daly was certainly more open and empathetic to priestly engagement with street issues, but I had little sense of him ever encouraging or facilitating discussion and exploration. In fact, because he was seen by both priests and people alike as the street priest par excellence, more of the political issues were diverted to him and his office. Many of the priests were more than happy for that to happen and Daly was more than happy to absorb and control that role. This unwillingness to talk and debate was one of the reasons that the Church's main contribution towards solutions for societal problems came from individual clergy rather from the institution itself, from individuals who would probably have been considered by their fellow priests as mavericks.

When I arrived in the cathedral parish in June 1970, the parochial house where the parish clergy lived was next door and attached to the bishop's house. I found it a fascinating place. Fr Benny O'Neill was the administrator and the minder, as well as adviser to the bishop. Because of the Troubles, O'Neill had gathered a small group of teachers and businessmen to be official consultants to the bishop. They were people of a certain age and of a similar cautious mindset to O'Neill himself. There was a tension between that group and the three priests who lived and worked in the cathedral parish.

Fr Tony Mulvey, Fr Eddie Daly and Fr John McCullagh had been curates in the cathedral parish for years and were active in a multitude of areas. Mulvey had established a housing association, which has grown into one of the largest in Northern Ireland. He had been influential, along with John Hume and others, in introducing the Credit Union movement to Derry. Reared in a political household himself, he was a close friend and quite often a provocateur to Hume. Daly, a music and drama producer of national stature, had an encyclopaedic knowledge of the families in his designated area of the parish. He was the priest who would become famous on Bloody Sunday after he was photographed waving a bloodied white handkerchief as he cleared a pathway for a dying youngster. A few years after I arrived, he would succeed Farren as bishop of Derry. Then there was McCullagh – writer, raconteur and advocate for those with physical and mental disabilities.

Those three experienced and highly regarded men were seldom consulted about what was happening on the streets. Statements were issued on behalf of the bishop without any input from any of them. Some of those public statements would have been contrary to what they would have thought but, more regularly and more frustratingly, often nothing was said when they believed a public statement should have been issued.

Mulvey was the one who taught me most on the streets. He was gruff and authoritative. He knew the people and he knew their history. He had strong but informed political opinions. On one of my first outings with him we were confronted by a group of young men waving a couple of Irish tricolours and intent on provoking a riot with the army. Mulvey asked them whether they knew Paddy Shields, a man who had been a leader of the IRA in Derry in the 1940s and 1950s. He quoted Shields as saying that the tricolour should never be used as a red rag to a bull. That was followed by a history lesson on the origins of the flag itself. By the time the lesson – accompanied by the challenge that their riotous actions were contributing nothing to the well-being of Ireland – had concluded, their enthusiasm for throwing stones at the army had evaporated.

Mulvey was also the priest who humbled me most. I had only been in the cathedral a few weeks, and was still in awe of my surrounds and the priests who served there, when he entered my room. He dropped to his knees in front of me and asked me to hear his confession. I was startled and embarrassed. Here was this older man and a priest of some stature putting himself in front of a rookie and revealing what he described as his sinfulness. He was the first to do this, but he was not the last. Several older priests during the following years did the same thing. I always found it humbling, and an insight into the depth of belief these men had in the sacramental life of the Church. I had a belief in sacramentality, but I don't think I ever had the depth of humility displayed by these men.

Eddie Daly used to tell a story about when I arrived in the cathedral. He and the other two curates, he claimed, started out slightly suspicious of me. Their boss, Fr O'Neill, in informing them that I was coming to help during the summer months, had boasted that I had been one of his altar boys and that I was the youngest of a good Catholic family from Buncrana, where he had served as a curate. Daly claimed that during my first weeks in Derry I was quiet and very respectful. Then, one evening, as the five of us sat around a dinner table, O'Neill, as he was wont to do, was excoriating the rioters of the previous night as being hooligans or communists or something of that ilk. As he was in full flight, Daly claimed, a voice that came from the bottom of the table said, 'Benny, that is a lot of crap.' Daly said that, apart from nearly choking on their chicken or whatever they were eating, the three curates knew that after that my days in the cathedral were numbered and I would be banished to some less auspicious parish. I don't recall the incident and it is possibly apocryphal, but I do remember the three curates becoming more open and warmer to me. I was transferred out of the cathedral that autumn.

The Long Tower parish, my new abode, was adjacent to the cathedral but ecclesiastically a million miles away. One clerical wag enjoyed saying that there were no golf courses in the Long Tower. Neither were there any in the cathedral parish, but it had stature and the presence of the bishop. But while most priests would have considered a move from there to the Long Tower a banishment, I loved my new parish. There were three other priests and two housekeepers in the parochial house. It was busy but, unlike the cathedral, none of those three priests had any interest in or desire to be engaging with what was happening in politics or in social change. They were pastorally active and always available to the people, but their response to the growing disturbance and violence on the streets was an appeal to pray for peace, accompanied by condemnation of violence.

Recently, I came across a long interview with me dated to February 1972, which reminds me of a few interesting events that took place in my early days in my new posting. It begins with me noting how the parish had been quiet and that I had spent my time getting to know its people. I had been designated to work with the young people of the parish on top of all my other normal duties. But that period of peace was soon broken on the night the first shots were fired in Derry.

I recalled how on that day I was at a meeting in the City Hotel addressing the problem of publicans who were selling drink to youngsters, mainly wine to twelve- to sixteen-year-olds. We were there, first and foremost, to find out how widespread this practice was – we knew it was going on, but we didn't know the extent of it. If it was widespread, we would see what could be done about it. Just as the meeting was coming to an end, John Hume came in and said that six to ten shots had been fired at the army. This would have been 7 July 1971, about a week prior to the shooting of Desmond Beattie and Seamus Cusack. I recalled in the interview:

> It was significant to me because afterwards I came to believe that the shooting was in some way planned. Things were too quiet, and it may have been an effort to increase the

tension, hoping that the army would react to it in some stupid way. And, of course, they reacted to it with open arms because a short time after that they shot and killed young Beattie and Cusack.

On the day Beattie and Cusack were killed, I had planned 'what was considered in Derry to be a fairly attractive football match'. This had been organised through the youth club and was to feature boys who had gone to England to play First and Second Division football; as I said, 'people who had made it in football, you know'. These boys were to play one of our local teams. The match had created quite a bit of interest and excitement. It was in the off season and 'it was going to be good'. We had a small stadium that had been closed down for repairs and this game was to mark its reopening, with a big dinner for later that evening accompanied by a band. It was going to be a good day for everyone, and it helped that we were going to make 'about 600 quid' for the youth club.

On the afternoon of the day in question, I had gone to check that everything had been set up for the match and the dance. I recalled, 'A young lad came to me and said, "A boy called Beattie has been shot." He had been shot by the army. I went down to see and there was fair riot going on, the worst with the army that I had seen to that point. It was bitter, very, very bitter.' Cusack had initially been brought to Letterkenny Hospital, but he died on the way there and his body was being brought back to Derry that evening, almost directly past the football pitch. It left me with a real problem:

Many were still thinking the match was on and the players had come from England. I just didn't know what to do, you know. So, we eventually decided to call off the dance and go on with the match, which we did. But obviously not many turned up for it. But anyway, as the day went on, things got worse and worse. There was a terrible tension all over the place. And, of course, this was followed later by a call from the SDLP [Social Democratic and Labour Party] for an enquiry, and its withdrawal from Stormont.

From that time on, you could almost see the thing escalating and sense that more and more people were going to be shot. The tension, bitterness and recrimination heightened with every killing.

In my recollection, the next significant event took place in August, the day internment was introduced. I recalled:

It was a very beautiful day and I arrived down in the Bogside and the Brandywell very early in the morning. I hadn't heard the trouble going on in the night or very early in the morning. I'm a very sound sleeper. But anyway, I arrived down in the Bogside to find that a lot of people had been lifted by the army that night. There was one old man called Barney Gilmore and I remember going over to his house and being told that they had really given Barney a lot of rough treatment. They fired a rubber bullet into his stomach and later he had to go through an operation. They were looking for his son John, who is now interned, but John wasn't there. He hadn't stayed in the house that night, so they lifted Barney and brought him in and let him out a couple of days later, when he went into hospital.

I spent most of the next three days in the Brandywell and Bogside area, just walking from house to house – I think I must have lost four pounds in those three days. At about one o'clock on the first day the women were at the doors shouting, 'internment has been introduced'.

> The next thing the IRA just appeared in force, and this was the first time they arrived, just walking around the streets with guns. There wasn't that many of them, of course, but they were there, they were visible, they wore masks. The thing I noticed was the newness of some of the guns. Now, I'm no expert on guns – I couldn't tell you what type they were, but I could tell you they were new.

I also noted that I didn't think the difference that internment made to the situation would ever be fully understood. In my mind it was a blunder that just couldn't be explained. It was also hard for anyone who didn't live somewhere like Derry or Belfast during that time to fully comprehend. For example, a lot of the boys aged sixteen and seventeen who had been in the youth club might have taken part in the odd riot prior to that, but in general they weren't much for such activities until suddenly it wasn't fun anymore. Internment made it serious – you could no longer be indifferent. As I noted in my interview, 'You had to be part of it, if you were part of that community.'

Yet, while tensions were increasing and the conflict growing more rooted and complex, humour and frivolity had not yet deserted the scene. Derry people have a spontaneous and often vicious sense of fun. Sociologists and psychologists would un-doubtably ascribe this to the years of deprivation, unemployment and poverty, but, whatever the source, I admired it greatly because it was so quick-witted and insightful, and it is a gift I don't possess.

However, even I have the odd quirky story to tell. Shortly after I arrived in the parish, I was the priest on call when the word arrived that an older man had been shot and a priest was needed. On driving to the incident, I was waved down by Leo Casey, who had been bursar in St Columb's College during my years as a student there. He lived in the parish and we had become friendly. He occasionally invited me to the Catholic Club, which was a social and drinking establishment for middle-class men. But this was an emergency, so I told Leo I had no time to talk to him but that if he went with me, we could talk afterwards. He got into the passenger seat and we continued on the short drive to the street where the shooting had happened.

Outside a house a small crowd had gathered, and an elderly man was half-sitting, half-lying on a step. He was in great distress and the people around him were saying he had been shot and needed to be taken to the hospital. I said I would drive him and asked that he be laid out on the back seat of my car. Leo said that he would go with me, but as he was about to climb into the back seat, a man I didn't know got in instead. As I drove speedily to the hospital, about two miles away and through two army checkpoints, it became clear that the man who had jumped in was quite drunk. As the elderly man moaned that he was so sore, the drunk man kept patting him on the head and telling him not to worry, that he was going to be fine. As I was pulling up to the hospital door a couple of paramedics appeared with a hospital trolley. Obviously, someone had telephoned ahead to the hospital. As the medics were lifting the wounded man from the car, he said to one of them, 'Maybe I haven't been shot. Maybe it's my piles.' I swear, it was the only time in thirty years that I said a silent prayer that someone *had* been shot.

It emerged afterwards that there had been a gun battle between the IRA and the army. A bullet had ricocheted off a wall and embedded itself in the soft tissue of the old man's backside. When I visited him a few days later, he was well on the mend and his piles were fine.

3

Adapting to the Times

IT IS WELL DOCUMENTED JUST how quickly human beings adapt to the abnormal. Guns, bombs, riots and killings were as foreign to me as they can ever be to a person. The only time I had carried a gun was a day's grouse shooting with a brother-in-law, who probably only invited me to ingratiate himself with my sister. I was in my early teens at the time and had no desire to replicate the experience as an adult. The kickback of the shotgun blackened my poor arm, and I could hardly move it for a week. Thankfully I missed every bird I shot at. Yet, I was surprised how quickly I did adapt.

Masses, baptisms, confessions, funerals, weddings, school visits, house visits and all the bits and pieces of parish life continued amongst the growing conflict and increasing violence. That mix became the norm for most priests, especially those in the city, and something similar but more disruptive and frightening was also the norm for many parishioners. But it would be shallow and misleading to describe it only in the negative. For those priests and laity who adapted to the new norm, there was a purposefulness to what was happening. It had an energy, an excitement, that was invigorating. Those who supported the civil rights campaign and the fewer, but still substantial, numbers who promoted and supported the violence, had a framework and a dynamic in their lives that might not have otherwise been there. The ones who suffered most were those who found all that was happening on the streets and in the political upheaval to be overwhelmingly hostile, frightening and futile. The longevity of what was happening, the repetitiveness of the Troubles, only increased their suffering.

It should also be remembered that all these happenings were taking place in the glare of the media. Notebooks, microphones and cameras were part and parcel of everyday life. Those of us who spent time on the streets were on first-name terms with journalists, cameramen and commentators. Within a couple of years, I had progressed from the terror of saying a few words to the local newspaper to frequently being interviewed by the Insight team of *The Sunday Times* or flying to London for *Panorama*. Priests had a uniform, they were traceable to the parish house, they were considered reasonably neutral and thus quotable by the growing number of media outlets covering the conflict. There was a limited number of politicians to talk to and, anyway, many of the media outlets preferred the voices of the ordinary man and woman telling their personal story. Even those who would not publicly participate felt some small pride in watching or listening to their neighbours on radio or television. It made them feel part of the narrative. We were being introduced to the paradox that conflict and danger can be invigorating and even life-enhancing.

On top of all that going on, I was still following advice I had been given by older priests even before the Troubles – that it was important to pay attention to one's own health by taking a day a week away from the parish and having a hobby or a recreational outlet. I played an occasional game of golf and attended most of the home games of the Derry City soccer team, which I had being doing with my two brothers since childhood. The football ground was in my parish. But even that was soon pulled into the cauldron of violence.

On a pleasant Saturday afternoon in September 1971, our team was playing Ballymena United at home. Towards the end of the match word came through the crowd that the visiting team's bus was being hijacked. With a few other supporters, I made my way to where it was happening. My impression was that it was a group of youngsters who were trying to get in on the act and gain some childish kudos from a violent protest. I sat on the ground in front of the bus, but there was enough space to drive safely around me, which they did. A few streets away from the ground, the bus was set alight. I was angry with the youngsters and annoyed that I had not arrived at the scene sooner, because I thought I would have been able to prevent the bus from being burned.

The consequence of this act was that Derry City were no longer allowed to play their home matches in the Brandywell. In hindsight, I could see that preventing the bus being burned might have postponed this action, but it would not have stopped it. Many of the other clubs were becoming frightened of entering the Bogside and there had been a long history of sectarian tensions between some of the clubs in the North. Derry City was ordered by the football authorities to play their home matches in Coleraine, a good hour's drive away. That lasted for a time but, without home support and the knock-on financial consequences, the club itself eventually withdrew from the league. I missed the matches and was saddened that the club had to stop playing for a good number of years.

When in Rome I had been introduced to wine and beer, but even though wine was an accompaniment to every meal, I was only ever an occasional drinker. Leo Casey, who had jumped into the car to go to the hospital with the man who was unsure about whether he had been shot, occasionally invited me for a drink in the Catholic Club. Initially I was uncomfortable, as I found the idea of a Catholic Club to be elitist, especially when I discovered that priests had automatic and free membership. However, I enjoyed the occasions because the company nearly always included Eddie McAteer and Stephen McGonagle.

McAteer had been leader of the Nationalist Party and a Member of Parliament who had only recently lost his seat to John Hume. McGonagle was a trade unionist who had stood for election against McAteer. I enjoyed their company and the conversation of these older political figures. It exposed me to the experiences of and insights from men who had been at the forefront of Northern Irish politics, who had suffered the frustration of contributing to public debate and intercourse over many years without, apparently, achieving any modicum of change. Despite their frustration and occasional anger, they were gracious, generous and philosophical, but every so often they revealed a hint of fearfulness, which I assumed arose from defeat after defeat, but which might also have been an educated premonition of the dangers of what was developing in Northern politics.

I was gradually becoming part of the Derry community. I was the youngest priest in the Long Tower parish and I wore a leather jacket. Whether it was my age or my gear, I received a lot of invitations to officiate at people's weddings. I really liked the wedding service and worked hard to make it meaningful. In the Catholic Church most marriage ceremonies are accompanied by a eucharistic celebration. The Second Vatican Council had adapted the ritual of the Mass to allow for a number of priests to concelebrate together, rather than each priest always celebrating on his own. I adopted some of that concelebration style, encouraging greater participation by the couple who were marrying each other, such as the bride and groom bringing the bread and wine to the altar, initially lighting two candles and, after the marriage ceremony itself, jointly lighting a single candle.

At that time anything outside of the strict codes was considered provocative and dangerous, and it wasn't long before I was told off by a senior cleric in the adjacent parish for ignoring, and even breaking, the rubrics of the Church, which he considered a serious issue. However, the brides and grooms liked it, and the wedding guests found it easier to engage with the ceremony. I also had the consolation that, within a few years, most of the priests in the diocese were similarly adapting the rubrics. These were the years when the rigidity of clerical correctness was slowly dissipating.

Weddings were good for getting to know people – a big day in anyone's life – but, like many priests, I came to dread the receptions. Hours waiting for hotels to serve a meal that was greatly inferior to what I would have become used to in the parochial house became a real pain and, eventually, I sometimes resorted to creating double appointments to avoid having to go.

Confessions were also constant and demanding, taking place in a small dark box, sometimes for hours at a time, *sotto voce*, with a person on the other side of a wire mesh – everything that is the antithesis of a human encounter, and yet some of the most important, instructive and, I believe, healing engagements took place there. Admittedly, much of it was formulaic and repetitive, but there was enough that was open and courageous and fragile and human. I did a lot of growing up in the confessional. When people open their hearts and reveal their problems, it becomes easier to know and understand your own heart. I also began to appreciate how much of a privilege it was that people would reveal their deepest feelings to a young and inexperienced man like me. I grew in knowledge and sensitivity to the human condition. Mostly, I fell in love with the people themselves.

The confession box may have been confined and formulaic, and the Catholic Church may have reduced the sacrament to an obsession with specific sins (mostly sexual), but, at its best and when done well, it was a magnificent facility for blending therapeutic and spiritual healing. The people who used the sacrament well taught me a lot about life and living, about relationships, about hardships and dreams, and about the innate goodness of most people. Mainly, but not exclusively, women allowed me, as a confessor, into the depths of their being. What was revealed was a mixture of hope and desolation. They were grateful to be able to talk and be listened to but had little knowledge of how much of a privilege I felt it was to be trusted to that degree. It was certainly exhausting, but the experience attracted me to therapy and counselling, and strangely enough to the art and the importance of politics.

On the streets, resentment to internment was still being felt. The IRA was growing in numbers and confidence and exploding bombs in the centre of the city. The civil rights movement had lost much of its momentum, with marches and rallies becoming a fading memory. Violence now claimed and dominated the streets. The civil rights leaders had coalesced into a political party – the SDLP, founded in August 1970. Gerry Fitt was its nominal leader, but in the eyes of Derry and many other places, John Hume was 'the man'.

This new political party gave some semblance of a voice and direction to the nationalist people, but it had no forum to which it could speak. As a response to internment and the killing by the British Army of young Beattie and Cusack, the SDLP had withdrawn from the already fragile political institutions. Moreover, the near unity that had been achieved among the nationalist community under the civil rights banner was being pulled apart. The divisions and tensions were increasing between those who believed and engaged in violence and those who believed that change should only be achieved by protest and politics.

One day would provide a microcosm of all the issues that were now present on the streets. It was 26 August 1971. The weather was beautiful. It was only a few weeks after internment had been introduced. On the way back from a meeting in the cathedral, I came across a confrontation between some locals and the British Army. It was not anything out of the ordinary in terms of shouting, stone-throwing and threats from the army that arrests would take place if the crowd did not disperse. Ivan Cooper and Hugh Logue, both members of the SDLP, were there, and for the next hour or more we were able to interpose ourselves between the army and the people and calm the situation until the small crowd eventually dispersed.

I had only driven a few streets when I ran into another, larger confrontation. It was clear that this one was more dangerous because there was no distance between the people and the army. I knew how dangerous that could be. A soldier, possessing a lethal weapon, can easily become isolated in such circumstances and, out of fear or anger, endanger himself and the crowd of people who are doing the confronting.

I managed to insert myself into the middle of the crowd and began talking to the soldier who seemed to be in command. The situation was as ugly as any I had ever witnessed. Some women were pulling caps and helmets off the heads of soldiers, and a few were spitting into their faces. I remember being impressed by the discipline of whatever regiment it was. Slowly, we managed to impose a small distance between the protesters and the soldiers. And then John Hume arrived. I was never as glad to see anyone in my life.

The army began to retreat with the crowd following, Hume and I between them. At some stage there was a scuffle and an army tank, or 'pig' as we called them, moved forward and hit Hume. He was dazed but not seriously hurt. His own home was not far from where the confrontation was happening, so a few locals took him there. I was now on my own for a short time. The army continued, very slowly, to reverse along the street until they reached the corner with Laburnum Terrace. By then Hume had returned, and once again I was very glad to see him.

Hume began talking to a senior officer who had also arrived on the scene. Years later I read a report that it was Paddy Ashdown, who went on to become leader of the British Liberal Party, but in those days, I would not have known who Ashdown was. Hume asked that the army withdraw from the area and said that he would then be able to get the crowd to disperse. However, the officer wanted to bring his men to the Creggan estate, half a mile from where we were, insisting that the crowd should disperse immediately. Following a heated discussion, Hume asked the crowd to sit down on the road. We all sat down. After a warning, the army brought a water-cannon tank and sprayed dyed water on the crowd. A water cannon has a lot of force and can knock you off your feet. Also, the blue dye in the water doesn't do clothes any favours.

I was put up against a wall by soldiers close to where Hume, along with Ivan Cooper and Hugh Logue, who had arrived shortly before the sit-down, were also spreadeagled. They were then led away to a Saracen tank, and I expected the same would happen to me. Instead, the soldiers just walked away and got into their tanks and lorries. They continued their journey to Creggan while I and the rest of the crowd were left behind with blue faces and very wet clothes. Hume and the others were taken to the local police station and detained for a few hours. Later that evening, on release, they were carried back into the Bogside on the shoulders of local people as heroes, restored to leadership on the streets and not just in the corridors of politics.

This event was important because it highlighted the dichotomy and the struggle between violence and peaceful protest, which was still present and unresolved at that time. There was a tug between the growing presence and the mounting activities of the IRA, and the appreciation and respect for the civil rights movement as embodied by Hume. It swayed back and forth and depended, to a great degree, on the latest actions or outrages committed by the army or the IRA – or, more accurately, on the two embodiments of the IRA, because the Official IRA, better known as 'the Stickies', was still active.

In the weeks and months before this event, it was felt that politics and Hume's leadership were being sidelined. The events of that day, however – the photographs of the peaceful protest, the dousing by the water cannon, and Hume and his fellow party members spreadeagled against a wall and carted off to the police station – tipped the scales of public sentiment, at least for a time, in favour of Hume and the new party that he and others had established.

Later that evening I called at Hume's house to see how he was after being hit by the tank and his sojourn in jail. He asked me to drive him to a local hotel where he was meeting some of his party members. I remember thinking that I would have loved to have gone into that meeting. I had become surer of my political footing, but the assumption was that priests and politics didn't mix and I understood and agreed with that. I do remember driving away, though, thinking it would have been nice to have been asked what I thought of what had happened that day and what consequences it might have. It was clear that the clash between peaceful protest and violence was increasing. The violence was gaining momentum and credence, particularly among the young, but there was still a strong residual support for non-violent protest. Even then I would have been conscious of how difficult it would have been to sustain peaceful protest, and I had seen enough to know how easily street protest can degenerate into violence. But I also suspected that taking the energy and the presence of the civil rights movement off the streets and transforming it into a mainstream political party was more than likely to leave the streets to the IRA and the British Army, and that would only have one outcome. It would ensure that there would be plenty of work for the priests.

In those days I wouldn't have been able to articulate the tensions as clearly as I would have wished, but I was becoming conscious of the dilemmas and the dangers. Having dropped

Hume off to attend his meeting, I drove back to the parochial house feeling a bit isolated and lonely. I had been on the streets from early morning, my mind and heart filled with all kinds of thoughts and feelings and no one with whom to share them. Even though I lived with a community of men, even though I ate at least two meals a day with them, and even though I liked them and came to greatly respect the administrator, Fr Willie McGaughey; despite all that physical closeness, I never felt that I could share my more personal views and feelings. I would not have come back and dropped into one of their rooms to talk about what had happened and how I felt about it.

In the heightened atmosphere of the Troubles and the high intensity of emotions that were part and parcel of each day's work, I felt an increasing need to talk, to explain and examine what was going on beneath the surface. I probably realised by then that men in general are not very good or comfortable with that type of openness. I knew that I wasn't great at it myself, but I was coming to realise that many of the priests I was encountering were particularly bad at it, even though they spent a good part of every day listening to the problems of other people. At a time when each priest in the Long Tower parish would have spent at least fourteen hours a week in a confessional box, listening to and absolving men, women and children of their sins, despite all of that, I would not have shared my feelings with them, nor they with me. That just seemed to be clerical culture. I had to wait another year or so before I found a soulmate in a priest to whom I could really talk.

The morning after the fracas on the Lone Moor Road, the newspapers were full of photographs of a very soaked John Hume and his fellow politicians. There must have been one of me also, because a photographer from one of the red-top English papers called to see me at the parochial house. He wanted to apologise for his paper's coverage of the previous day's events. He had sent in some photographs with a caption describing protesters, including me, being sprayed with water by the army. A sub-editor had replaced his word 'protesters' with the word 'rioters'. It may only have been the difference of one word, but there is a political gap as big as a chasm between those two concepts. In the context of the struggle between violence and peaceful protest that was being played out on the streets of Derry, language was also a weapon.

This incident taught me more about the how the media worked. The British media was not going to report the subtleties or the complexity of what was happening in places like the Bogside. An overly simplistic and biased account was easier and maybe more acceptable to its readership. But, in fairness, they were not the only ones who were not seeing the events in the way that I saw them.

A few days after the confrontation on the Lone Moor Road, I got a phone call from the bishop's house asking me to go to see him. He had received a letter complaining of my engagement on the streets. I was still young, shy and nervous about a meeting with the bishop. It was clear that he was not overly pleased with my behaviour, but he quickly let it drop that the letter was anonymous, which allowed me to assert that such letters should not be entertained. That put him on the back foot. It was a short meeting, and I didn't feel as chastised as I would have anticipated.

Out of the meeting in the local hotel at which I had dropped John Hume came the announcement that there would be a public rally in the Brandywell football ground the following week. The publicity of Hume's dousing with water and his arrest ensured that a very large crowd attended. It must have been a good summer that year because I remember sitting on the grass in the middle of the football pitch. The SDLP was already in civil disobedience mode and this rally was a further opportunity to display and vent the anger that internment had induced, but it was also an opportunity to reassert the primacy of politics and non-violent protest in the face of the heightened presence and actions of the IRA.

When the announcement came from the platform that the SDLP was asking the public to stop paying rates and rent to the local authorities, I was excited and saw an opportunity for a strong community mobilisation, the establishment of structures to collect the money into a communal fund and devising ways of spending the interest that would be generated from the accumulated collection. My mind was racing, wondering how Saul Alinsky or Cesar Chavez would avail of such an opportunity. How would they best organise such a strike and to what best purposes would they dedicate the money? I was assuming that the money would be paid back at some time in the future.

I remember how disappointed and angry I felt when it became clear that the money would not be collected. John Whale, one of the famous *Sunday Times* Insight team, was spending a lot of time in Derry in those days and, with Peter Pringle and others, was regularly publishing articles on the worsening political impasse in the North. Whale must have heard that I was unhappy with the decision to stage a rate and rent strike without any attendant infrastructure because he arrived at the parochial house asking for an interview. He ran a piece in *The Sunday Times* the following

Sunday with a quote from me about my disagreement with the strategy.

I was now convinced that the only way to challenge and resist both the IRA and the British Army was to inhibit and marginalise them on the streets. The only way that could have traction would be to mobilise the local community. For a few years that community had responded to the demand for civil rights by publicly protesting. While street protests have a shelf life and carry inherent dangers, to withdraw too quickly and too drastically would inevitably leave a vacuum that would be filled by militancy. Some form of alternative and graduated protest to bridge the movement to party politics taking place would not be easy and probably not sustainable, but it would be a more creative response than creating a vacuum. The rent and rates strike was good for the political party, but it would leave the people twiddling their thumbs. I wanted something more, such as job creation, skills training and for adult education schemes to be established. I considered that a glorious opportunity to do something meaningful with the authority and the backing of the party to which the people had given their support, and with the monetary interest that could accrue from the strike, was being passed up, and I was far from happy about it.

I was even more unhappy when, years later, one of the political leaders who had been on the stage at that open-air meeting in the Brandywell, Austin Curry, became the SDLP Minister for Housing in the devolved government and announced that people not only were obliged to pay their arrears of rates and rent, but that they would face prosecution if they failed to do so. I thought I might have been the only person to remember the details of that day, until the present leader of the SDLP, Colum Eastwood, told me recently that at every election in which he had canvassed, some voters would angrily confront him about the rates and rent strike and the way the people had been duped and betrayed. I was glad that there were others who still remembered.

4

The Awfulness of Violence

NOTHING STAYED STATIC IN THOSE days. Despite the efforts
to redirect protests into politics and to keep the streets free from
violence, one or other of the combatants had the ability to upset
any fragile equilibrium.

In the first three years of my time in the parish, I was introduced to the awfulness of violence. It was painful to experience
the destruction it inflicts on a family and a community but also to
witness the deception and degradation that is inevitably generated
in the use and in the justification of violence. The killings that
happened in or around my parish between the autumns of 1971
and 1973 were indicative of the deaths that would happen over
the next forty years. During those two years, there were killings
that led up to and killings that arose out of the awfulness and
the transformative impact of Bloody Sunday. Every experience
of death and killing is indelible in its impact, but Bloody Sunday
stands out as seminal in the history of this time and indeed, in
some of the decisions I would eventually make in the face of the
continuing and growing violence. However, my first encounter
with violent death came before this and even though those killings

were less public, less written about, they also left a lasting mark on my thinking.

The first of those killings was by the British Army on 15 September 1971. I hadn't known Billy McGreanery all that well or for all that long. We hadn't had time to get to know each other intimately, but we knew enough to realise that we liked each other. He worked in a shop at the edge of the parish – a shoe shop, if my memory is accurate. I had first met him during my few short months in the cathedral, and we would have run into each other, on and off, around the town.

Observers said that he had got out of a car and begun to walk towards his home, which was nearby, when he was shot. I remember the shock of it. But I remember even more the news bulletin that went out, within the hour, on all the media outlets. It was a time before killings became a daily occurrence and a daily news item. The news bulletin said that a gunman had been shot and killed by the army in the Lone Moor area of Londonderry, the same area where the sit-down protest with John Hume and the water-cannon spraying had taken place less than a fortnight earlier. The gunman, the radio and television reports said, had been firing at the army before being shot dead.

I still remember the anger I felt. I would have been angry enough at Billy's death, but to hear a public announcement that described him as a gunman who had been shot dead because he was shooting at the army left me feeling outraged. I didn't know everyone who was in the IRA, but I knew who was *not* in the IRA. Billy McGreanery was as likely to be in the IRA as I was. The suggestion of him carrying and firing a gun was preposterous. But the propaganda war had already begun, and Billy was one of its first victims. Those who didn't already know, me included, were learning that there was a massive publicity machine behind the British Army and British security. Facts were to be controlled and even manipulated to suit the narrative that put the army and government in the best possible light.

It would have been bad enough if the story that day had been that a man had been shot in Derry and that the police were investigating or there was a call for witnesses. But, instead, Billy McGreanery, as modest and decent a man as you would wish to know, a man of outstanding character, was now a gunman, and that would be the story and the belief for years to come for those who only knew or cared about what they heard on radio or television.

It was forty years before that slur was removed from the public record. Forty years before the army was forced to publish a public apology. In September 2011 the BBC reported:

> The Chief of the General Staff of the British Army has sent an official apology to the family of a man shot dead by a soldier in Londonderry.
>
> Billy McGreanery, 41, was killed by a member of the 1st Battalion Grenadier Guards in 1971.
>
> In June, the Historical Enquiries Team found he 'was not carrying a firearm and he posed no threat to the soldiers'.
>
> In his letter, Sir Peter Wall said an official apology was right and proper.
>
> He said that the soldier who shot him 'was mistaken in the belief that he had a weapon and this error, tragically, resulted in the death of an innocent man'.
>
> His family acknowledged the apology but said it was too late for those closest to Mr McGreanery ...

'The MoD have acknowledged that Billy ... was a totally innocent man who posed no threat. We feel we have finally set the truth free and somewhat righted a terrible wrong,' they said.

At the time of the shooting, the RUC chief superintendent in the city, Frank Lagan, recommended that the soldier responsible should have been charged with murder.

Mr McGreanery was killed at the junction of Eastway, Lonemoor Road and Westland Street on 15 September 1971.

Soldier 'A' was never prosecuted, on the advice of the attorney general, who said 'whether he acted wrongly or not, the soldier was at all times acting in the course of his duty'.

While it was welcomed that the lies told at the time were over-thrown and that an apology, belated as it was, was published, I was fascinated by the attorney general's statement: whether the soldier acted rightly or wrongly, this was done in 'the course of his duty'. That comes close to saying 'anything goes' or 'shoot to kill' as long as it can be included in 'the course of duty'. That type of response and excuse for unacceptable actions was what soured the relationship between the army and locals, who had initially and not all that long before this murder offered a warm welcome to the soldiers on their arrival. There is also the reference to Chief Superintendent Frank Lagan recommending that the soldier should be prosecuted for his actions. Despite this recommendation that did not happen, and I think I am right in saying that no soldier was ever prosecuted in those years.

By this time Frank Lagan was playing an increasing role in my life and would continue to do so in the following few years before he resigned from the RUC and I from the priesthood. He was in a powerful position, but he was as frustrated as I and others were. All his efforts at keeping a lid on an explosive situation were being outdone and overrun by the efforts and the momentum of the two main combatants. The IRA used violence to drive home their demand for a united Ireland and the British security forces used violence to defeat those who used violence to achieve their objective. Behind these two forces there was little political understanding and less political momentum to define and address the problem.

The unnecessary shooting and death of Billy McGreanery was a tragedy which captured that frustration and powerlessness. Frank Lagan would not have known Billy, but he knew the people who knew him, and he knew from their testimony that Billy was a completely innocent man who was unjustifiably shot dead, probably by a nervous or trigger-happy soldier. Lagan was able to lodge his recommendation that the soldier be prosecuted, and he was by far the most influential person within the political structures, but he felt powerless in bringing about political engagement and negotiation between the two main combatants who were militarily facing up to each other with increasing ferocity, which was inevitably going to result in more deaths like Billy's.

A tall, thin, slightly austere man, Lagan oversaw policing within the Derry district and eventually became an assistant chief constable. He was a practising Catholic, which should have been an irrelevance, but because there were few Catholics within the police at that time, about 8 per cent of the total, and there was growing antagonism between the Catholic community and the police, his religious affiliation was noted and noteworthy. He was holding down an important but near impossible role. His knowledge of the Catholic and nationalist community, and their historic and increasing antagonism to the RUC, left him juggling extremely sensitive and complex issues. He managed as well as anyone could have, helped greatly by having a network of people across the city and district whom he used as consorts and first responders. I was one of that network. In fact, Lagan would be the originator and, in some manner, the fourth member of the backchannel with which I later became involved.

'Community policing' is part of the jargon of modern police forces, but Lagan had perfected it in Derry long before it became fashionable. Even though the organisation that he led had little support among most of the inhabitants, and the district that he was policing was a war zone, he had tentacles in every part of the community, feeding and being fed the concerns of the people. Phone calls from him were common, enquiring what was happening in a street, or requesting that some of us should go to a part of the parish to prevent or calm a riot. At other times it was to ask us to go to a family to tell them that their son or daughter had been arrested. He had at least one priest in every parish and in some of the larger parishes two or three with whom he kept in regular contact. He had the same relationship with politicians, councillors and community workers, and was regularly on the phone trying to prevent trouble or calming the consequences of an unfortunate event.

After his death in 2005, I did an interview for the local radio in which I recounted an incident when he rang me to say that he had intelligence that the IRA were planning an ambush on police officers. I think it was the summer of 1971, because the location of the ambush was to be the grounds of Magee College, which was empty of students for the summer months. The time and place were known to Special Branch, but, despite the threat to their colleagues' lives, they were not going to intervene because that would expose one of their informants. What was little understood in those early days, and indeed throughout the Troubles, were the internal tensions and rivalries that existed between the different branches of the security forces. To the local nationalist people the only difference between the army and the police was the uniform they wore. Detectives, Special Branch and uniformed police were all the same – some wore a uniform, some didn't. MI5 and MI6 were spies, spooks, James Bond characters, who you could see on the screen in the cinema but who had no presence or relevance in our Troubles. The intricacies of conflicting security politics were beyond our interest and, in those days, beyond our understanding. Not surprisingly, given their attitude to this attack, the relationship between Lagan and Special Branch – the arm of policing that, years later, the Patten Report described as a force within a force – was not good at the time and would get worse in the following years. There appeared to be an ongoing battle between Lagan and the head of the local Special Branch unit.

On this occasion, Lagan asked me to try to get the IRA to call off the attack. I can't remember to whom I spoke, it could have been any one of four or five people. It would not have taken long to make contact because the IRA had a house within the parish that was considered their headquarters. Those were the days of 'Free Derry', the days when the IRA was openly operating within the area known as the Bogside, at least during daylight hours. After dark was different, as that was when the British Army would make sorties into the area. Thankfully, that ambush didn't happen. By this time, I had become quite cynical and questioning. Did something happen because I had intervened, or were there other forces at work of which I had little knowledge?

I suspected that Lagan's reputation within the RUC was different to the one he held among those of us who worked on the ground in Derry. Certainly, the priests and the local politicians held him in high regard for the efforts he consistently made to keep a lid on a very volatile situation. However, I doubt that the same positive opinion of him would have been held by some of his senior colleagues within the RUC. I suspect that he didn't have the full support of the more senior police officers he worked with as he was probably considered to be too sympathetic to the nationalist and republican ideology. Once or twice, when I became vice chair of the Policing Board, I raised his name with senior police colleagues and I detected a hesitation, even a reluctance, to praise his efforts. Years later, after he was long retired, I tried to get him to reminisce about his time in the police. In the little he said, I never once heard him criticise or bad-mouth his former colleagues, and there was always a sympathetic understanding of how difficult those years were for those who served in the RUC.

Frank Lagan was extremely focused on the politics of policing and security, something of which I had little or no knowledge in those early days of the Troubles. I also had little understanding of his argument that the RUC should not be in the primary role of responding to the security situation and should not be in the front line against the IRA and the various manifestations of loyalist paramilitaries. Lagan argued that the RUC placed in that role made them a paramilitary organisation rather than a police service. I didn't pay much attention to the argument and took the accepted view that the army and the police were much of a muchness.

Years later, on taking up the role on the new Policing Board, I came to a greater appreciation of Lagan's argument even though

I knew by then that he was a man before his time. Being 'before your time' in politics and life is a position that is much more difficult and frustrating than being behind the times. He tried to moderate and inform the entrenched security view that the Troubles were instigated and perpetuated by criminal elements within the North. That narrative dominated the security services and helped influence and ultimately dictate the political position within Westminster and even Dublin. Despite Lagan's best efforts, the analysis that all paramilitary organisations involved in the Troubles were criminals who should be dealt with within the normal criminal justice processes became the dominant policy position. It became formalised when Roy Mason became secretary of state for Northern Ireland in 1976 and Kenneth Newman was appointed chief constable of the RUC. Shortly after their appointments and the implementation of that policy, Lagan resigned from the RUC.

This was a disastrous policy that prolonged the conflict and resulted in the hunger strikes of the early 1980s. It also did immense harm to the police, initially separating them further from the nationalist community and gradually from the unionist working-class community where the loyalist paramilitaries had their roots.

Not all that many months after Billy McGreanery was killed, Lagan was faced with a decision that was taken above his head: to introduce the Parachute Regiment onto the streets of Derry. It is clear from the Saville Tribunal into the events of Bloody Sunday that Lagan had proposed that the civil-rights march planned for that day be permitted to proceed to the Guildhall, the intended destination of the march, and that cautions and arrests, if necessary, take place post-event. Had that advice been accepted, there may have been no deaths on that terrible day and history might have been somewhat different to what we went on to experience for the next forty years.

Lagan's evidence to the Saville Inquiry, evidence which was not disputed, did not receive the attention it deserved. Years later, I sat for three days in a room in London being briefed by a senior police officer who had access to most of the security files of those years. His view was that the tragedy of the Troubles was not that there was a grand conspiracy policy by the British government, but rather that there was no policy at all. The senior police officer who had 'lived' with the security files for the greater part of twenty years described it as 'ad hoc(ery) gone mad'. When he said that, I thought of Frank Lagan and his efforts.

5

Bloody Sunday

BLOODY SUNDAY WAS A MASSACRE. That is what I told the British Army chaplain I met on my way back from the killings. It was a huge event in the lives of those who were present, huge in the history of Derry and huge in the trajectory of the Troubles. I saw some of the killings carried out by the Parachute Regiment first hand. I anointed and prayed over some of the dead. I gave witness at two separate judicial inquiries.

I remember vividly most of the things that I witnessed during the twenty minutes in which the shooting and killing took place, but there are still small gaps in my memory that I have never been able to fill. I remember being frogmarched by paratroopers down an alleyway with a group of men who were loaded into trucks or Saracens and driven away. I remember an officer shouting to a soldier to release me, to let 'the padre' go.

However, I cannot remember how I got from the alleyway to the opposite side of Rossville Street, where I met Fr Mulvey. There are photographs of him and me beside an ambulance. I cannot remember how or where I met the British Army chaplain, but there is a contemporaneous statement from me about that meeting, recording how I said to him that what had happened was a massacre.

I nearly didn't go on the civil rights march that was taking place that day. That Sunday was my turn to officiate at the child baptisms scheduled for the same time as the march. I was also undecided about the wisdom of the march itself. John Hume had refused to endorse it. A week earlier, Saturday 22 January, he had led an anti-internment protest on Magilligan beach, not far from the city. The Parachute Regiment had blocked the march, fired rubber bullets and tear gas into the crowd, and had been quite disrespectful to Hume in a verbal tussle about its legality, all of which was captured by television cameras. Hume had said publicly, after that incident, that he was worried about a possible confrontation with the same regiment on narrow city streets and that it would be better if the planned march didn't take place.

From early on the morning of 30 January, the army had partially sealed off the Bogside with barbed wire and checkpoints. People coming and going to the five Masses that took place in the Long Tower parish on a Sunday morning reported that it was difficult to get to the church because of the very heavy presence of the army and the blockades that they had erected on all the roads into the area. The atmosphere was tense and many people to whom I talked were annoyed at the heavy and intimidating army presence – this may have ensured, rather than prevented, a large crowd attending the march.

Despite my initial indecision, after the baptisms I wandered down to the William Street area, where the march had already been stopped by the army from proceeding to its planned destination at the Guildhall and where rioting was just breaking out. I wandered amongst the crowd for about a half hour, chatting to people I knew, but then, weary of another riot, began to walk back to the parochial house. As I passed through Glenfada Park, I heard gunshots and saw crowds of people fleeing towards Free Derry corner. Several men came running into Glenfada carrying a young man. It was obvious that he had been shot. I ran to them, and they laid him on the ground where I knelt and said a few prayers. By then, the shooting had increased into an uninterrupted volley, and I became aware of a group of people taking shelter against one of the gable walls. As I finished the mouthful of prayers, the young men carried the wounded boy away towards what they hoped was a safer place and I ran to the gable wall.

Yards from the wall was a kind of barricade, which was really just a rubble of stones, and beside those stones were three bodies. At least one was alive because an arm was intermittently raised and lowered. It is the instinct of a priest to be beside a dying person. I was near but not beside, and I think I knew that if I went to them, I would die. I made a movement that someone else taking shelter at the gable wall wrongly interpreted as me starting to go to the three men, so he rushed to hold me back.

I remember thinking that it was strange that you could see a bullet, in the sense that when it hit the ground you could see its movement. This held a horrible fascination for me because I had a dread of being shot in the head. As I heard the bullets flying, I could see little bits of dust rising – the bullets were bouncing either just north or just south of the rubble barricade. They were coming from where the soldiers were, and even in those early days of the Troubles, most of us could distinguish the sound of British Army gunfire from IRA gunfire. While our shelter behind the gable wall was safe, outside the gable end was not, so we remained there for I have no idea how long. It could have been an eternity or seconds.

Then the Paras came into Glenfada Park. Big, aggressive men with blackened faces. One kept shooting, spraying bullets indiscriminately. They appeared surprised to see the group of us huddled against the wall and ordered us to put our hands on our heads and walk towards William Street. One of them kept shooting and as I grabbed his arm to stop him, he threw me to the ground. It was only then I noticed other bodies lying on the ground in the park. Shouted at again to put our hands on our heads and walk, all of us in the group were frogmarched towards William Street and eventually spreadeagled against a wall and told that we were under arrest. An army lorry arrived, and we were ordered onto it before the officer shouted to let 'the padre' go. I have always hated that word, 'padre'.

I staggered back towards Glenfada Park, coming across other bodies and being told by bystanders that other priests had anointed and prayed with the dead. I think I went into shock around then because my memory is less vivid and trustworthy after this, and I still cannot remember how and when I crossed Rossville Street and met up with Fr Tony Mulvey. It was years later that I read and only vaguely remembered my own statement that I had met the army chaplain after the shooting had stopped. After my massacre comment, he had said that we should say an 'Our Father' together, and that I was glad of that.

People still talk of the silence that fell over the city on the night and in the days that followed Bloody Sunday. A hush – a shared feeling that words, even quiet talk, would sound like clatter. The only comfort was to move from house to house and sit quietly by the coffins of those who had been shot dead. That hush lasted as the thirteen coffins were lined up a few days later, side by side in the church that overlooked the city, and then parted as each family carried their dead to their place of rest.

In the days after Bloody Sunday hundreds of men and women, maybe thousands, made quiet resolutions to themselves that they would do whatever and as much as they could to ensure that those who were killed would get some form of justice. There was a resolve that the world would know that these were completely innocent people who were shot down in cold blood while walking and protesting on their own streets. That those in authority who decided to use the Paratroopers, famous for only ever shooting to kill, and the Paras themselves, who willingly pulled the trigger, would somehow and someday be charged with the murders they had committed in broad daylight.

For forty years or more those people attended the short prayer service that took place on the morning of each anniversary. Or they joined every march that followed the original route on the afternoon of each 30 January. If they were in other parts of Ireland, or indeed in other parts of the world, they kept an ear to the happenings and to the families of Bloody Sunday. They quietly wished those families well and hoped for a righting of the wrongs done on that awful day.

The Widgery Tribunal, which the British government established to inquire into the events of the day and the deaths that took place, only rubbed salt into the wounds. After a very perfunctory examination and calling only a handful of witnesses, despite thousands of people having witnessed what had happened and providing written statements, Widgery came close to justifying the killings, accusing the Paras of little more than carelessness, and putting much of the responsibility for the thirteen deaths and the many injuries on the organisers and those who participated in the march.

Ominously, Bloody Sunday created momentum for the Provisional IRA. It put the British government onto the defensive and in the following years, instead of it acting as an impartial broker, it ended up fighting a guerrilla group rather than solving a political problem. We have all had to live with that, and the people who have died since have suffered the consequences.

The families of those who were killed on that day, with the help of the Irish government, local politicians and civic leaders, fought for years to have the Widgery Tribunal findings overturned. Eventually, in 1998, in the early years of the peace process, the British agreed to demands for a new inquiry and appointed a high court judge, Lord Saville, to chair the inquiry, with the assistance of a judge from Canada and one from New Zealand.

I was not a total admirer of the Saville Inquiry. On the positive side, it delivered judgements that established the innocence of the dead and forced the British government to deliver an apology to the families of those killed and injured. Its findings helped firm up the peace process and enhanced the atmosphere of reconciliation that was embryonic at the time. Those were major achievements. On the negative side, however, it took too long, cost too much and was weak on the political analysis of why the massacre was allowed to happen and the learning that should have arisen from what David Cameron, the then prime minister, called the 'unjustified and unjustifiable' killings that took place.

I attended the first day of the Saville Tribunal in the Guildhall in Derry. The Great Hall is impressive in décor and size, and on that day and every day for almost two years there was row after row of solicitors and barristers. On that first day I was asked for a comment from a local TV station and said that I found the setting off-putting and intimidating. The bank of solicitors and barristers sitting below three judges raised high on a platform looked more like a court of law than an inquiry at which hundreds of witnesses, the ordinary men and women of Derry, could relate their story.

On 15 June 2010, nine years after its first sitting, the tribunal issued its findings and proclaimed the dead and injured of Bloody Sunday innocent, posing no threat to the people who killed them. On that day most of the people who had given evidence, and those who had supported the families during their long quest to establish the injustice that had been committed, felt that their quiet resolution had led to their duty being discharged. At such a time distance from the event, the talk of charging and jailing soldiers was a matter they would leave to the families themselves and to those who had greater legal and political experience of things like that.

The families' reactions were mixed. All of them viewed the Saville Report as cathartic but not all saw it as the final resolution. Some considered it an important step in achieving the prosecution of the soldier who had killed their loved one, others as the resolution they desired, while still others considered the possibility of murder charges against soldiers as being unlikely because of the time gap and the sparsity of forensic evidence taken on the day.

That layering of responses – wanting prosecutions, not wanting prosecutions, wanting information and truth only, wanting recognition and compensation – is to be found in every aspect of our legacy. It is not peculiar to the Bloody Sunday killings. It is to be found among most of the victims and survivors of our 'Troubles'. It is also reflective of the feelings of civic society, where a growing number think that enough attention has been given to the past and that it is time to draw a line under it.

After the findings of the Saville Inquiry, expectations had mounted that at least three, and possibly four, soldiers would be charged with murder. Amongst themselves, the media moved their expectations to the next stage in the saga – how the prosecutions of former paratroopers would create an uproar across the water in Westminster, where the Conservative Party was already talking of changing the law to ensure that former soldiers would be free from prosecution. So far only Soldier F has been charged with two murders and his prosecution is ongoing.

The fallout from Bloody Sunday was massive and is well-documented elsewhere. But at the time, the days and weeks after the killings, the normal equanimity of the clerical world was also interrupted, at least for a time. Tellingly, there were seven or eight priests present on the day itself and a very quick decision was made by them to call a press conference. That coming together of ordinary parish priests and curates was both rare and interesting. A quick meeting was called in advance to decide what would be said and who would say it. I found the coming together of older and younger priests, even for that short time, very supportive and comforting. There was no talk of referring matters to the bishop or anyone else. This group had communally experienced something shocking and evil, and we were determined that nothing or no one would stand in the way of us expressing our abhorrence of those deaths and the manner of the executions. Bishop Neil Farren, who would normally have dictated the response to such an event, was frail and incapable of a coherent response. But even had he been in his full health and authority, the anger and the responsibility that the priests felt would not have been corralled. At the press conference the priests told their stories and collectively accused the British government of murder. I think that was the first time I ever spoke at such an event.

All of the priests at the press conference would have gone to each of the houses of those killed, irrespective of the city parish to which the deceased was attached. Fr Tom O'Gara and Fr Eddie Daly were already in one of those houses, five storeys up in the Rossville flats, the only high-rise flats in Derry, when I arrived. At that time O'Gara and I were becoming friends. He and I had attended St Columb's College at the same time – he as a day boy, I as a boarder – but we didn't know each other during those years. He was ordained a year after me, had been sent to Maynooth Seminary and then was appointed to teach mathematics in St Columb's College, situated in the Long Tower parish where I was working.

The wake house in which we all met was in the area of the cathedral parish that Eddie Daly officially visited. He was already well known in the city, but, on this day, he was becoming well known throughout Ireland and much further afield as the priest caught on camera waving a white handkerchief in front of a group of men carrying young Jackie Duddy, who had been shot dead while running away from the British Army. Those pictures were being shown on televisions all over the world.

Daly and O'Gara nodded as I entered the wake house. I didn't know the family, so it was a relief that Daly was there. He was a meticulous visitor of homes. Every weekday afternoon he would set out from the cathedral to call to six or seven houses.

I knew this from my time living with him in the cathedral house the previous summer. His visitation book was kept like a sacred script, meticulous in detail, but well fingered by constant usage. I was in awe and slightly jealous of his self-discipline, a quality I lacked.

I was also pleased that O'Gara was there. The walls of St Columb's were beginning to feel like a prison to him, so he spent every free afternoon and night out in the city parishes. We had been spending some time together and were discovering that the priests we worked with were somewhat of an enigma to both of us. Hardworking and committed, most of them knew their parishes like the back of their hands. A few were haughty and patronising to their parishioners, but the bulk were compassionate, generous and dedicated. Most were understanding and protective of 'their people', as they called them, and were increasingly available, day and night, as the strife and the violence on the streets was growing in frequency and intensity. At that pastoral level, they were everything and more than anyone could have asked for or expected. But many, maybe most, were reluctant to move beyond that pastoral role. Despite the very strong statement made at the press conference accusing the British government of murder, they were reluctant to engage in the social implications of what was happening in the city and across Northern Ireland, and were loath to even discuss, never mind engage in, the political ramifications.

O'Gara hadn't spoken very much when we were in the wake house. That didn't surprise me. I had known him to sit in houses for hours, slowly getting to know the family. That morning, the three of us talked for a time, standing outside on the fifth-storey balcony overlooking the streets and alleyways where most of the killings had taken place. Eddie Daly told us that the Irish government had already asked him to go to America. They wanted him to undertake an extensive tour of the States, making himself available to the American media. The British propaganda machine was in overdrive, according to the Irish, and a priest who had been present and seen the actions of the British paratroopers could relay the truth of what had happened and counteract the propaganda.

O'Gara did not respond with the enthusiasm that Daly might have expected. I knew that he would have been quietly sceptical of America's importance and the usefulness of pitting propaganda against propaganda. I had a foot in both camps – not against the idea of Daly going to America, but more of a mind that the most important work had to be done at home, in Derry. I was standing with Tom on my left and Eddie on my right, me in the middle, thinking that it was the appropriate place for me because there were aspects of both men in me. I had some of Tom's empathetic reflectiveness, but I also had a lot of Eddie's pragmatism. It was an uncomfortable conversation. Eddie was probably expecting enthusiasm and encouragement from us, but what he got was hesitancy, some from me, more from Tom. If I had been asked, I would probably have gone to America while thinking that Tom, like Mary in the gospel story of Lazarus, had chosen the better part. A few days later, Eddie went off on his tour, while Tom sat night after night in the homes of some of the families of the Bloody Sunday dead. I was left to handle the BBC.

6

Conversations

DAVID FROST WAS PROBABLY THE best-known presenter on the BBC at that time. His producer got in touch with me, asking for help with a live programme from Derry on the events of Bloody Sunday that Frost would present. He wanted me to find a venue and thirty to forty people to take part in the programme and to ensure that equipment and crew would be secure and safe in the highly volatile days after Bloody Sunday. I agreed.

The venue I showed him, which he agreed to use, was the Lourdes Hall, the parish youth club that doubled up two nights a week as a bingo venue. There was no problem in rounding up thirty to forty people who were willing to talk about what had happened. Then, two nights before the programme was broadcast, I was informed that the venue was unsuitable and the show was being moved to a more neutral location, a school in a more middle-class area of Derry. On the day of the broadcast, I discovered that half of the programme would be coming from Derry and half from Belfast, from the Shankill Road. I was told this would make it a more balanced broadcast. It wasn't difficult to read the embarrassment in the producer's eyes and to realise that political pressure from some quarter in the bowels of British politics had kicked in.

David Frost arrived on the morning that the programme was due to be aired. I was so angry that I don't think I even said hello or offered him any kind of welcome. It was an awful programme, a pitting of a loyalist community who had little knowledge of Derry and less of the event itself again a nationalist/republican community who were still in shock and still grieving. It taught me that the word balance, beloved by the media, is no guarantee against imbalance.

In the days following Bloody Sunday and up to the Widgery Tribunal in February and March of that year, there were more conversations between priests in the Derry area than at any other period of the Troubles. After the priests' press conference, there was a further coming together to debate whether to give evidence to the Widgery Tribunal, which had been promised by the British government in response to international pressure. That debate was intense and painful. There was an understanding that the public and probably the families of the dead and injured would follow the lead of the priests. Not to go and give evidence might appear to undermine the strong eyewitness testimony that the priests and many others had delivered in public. But to go and give testimony was to put the hopes and the expectations of a hurt community into the hands of a British judge, who was not even prepared to take evidence in the city where the crime had been committed. Witnesses would have to travel to Coleraine to be heard. Not a good portent. However, the decision was taken to co-operate with the tribunal, and while it was probably the wrong decision, it was taken in good faith and with the full agreement of the priests who had been present on the streets on that awful Sunday.

Underpinning these conversations was a more pressing question – one that got little airing among the clergy themselves – on the role that the Church and the priest should fulfil moving forward. If it was true, as it obviously was, that we were no longer in the twilight world between civil rights protests and violence, but in the foothills of an all-out war between the Provisional IRA and the British state, then the Church(es) would be challenged about responses to that frightening reality. Yet, apart from Tom O'Gara and myself talking about it on a weekly basis, I was aware of no formal or organised conversations among the clergy in the diocese. As we two were among the most junior priests in the diocese, our thoughts, in a hierarchical Church, would count for nothing.

If it hadn't been so pathetic, an incident that happened to Tom and me in those early years of priesthood could be considered mildly comical, if also a significant confirmation of the Irish clerical world's deep reluctance to engage with what was happening in the North. The Irish bishops decided that the young clergy needed a theological and pastoral refresher. There was a reference to a fall-off in theological and canonical discipline among the younger priests. We were instructed to meet in the Columban seminary in Navan, where some lectures were delivered by one of the Irish bishops, whose name I cannot remember, and by some university lecturers and clerics. These lectures were followed by discussion.

On the second day, Tom got to his feet and in his usual passionate and challenging manner asked how it could be that fifty or sixty miles up the road there was a political, social and religious revolution happening, which had not been mentioned even once in the proceedings. The reaction was instructive. Silence, discomfort, embarrassment. The audience was roughly one-third northern and two-thirds from the southern dioceses. It was hard to know who was the most discommoded and the least willing to respond to Tom's challenge.

Shortly after Tom's intervention, I was approached by the administrator of the event, who had been a few years ahead of me in the Irish College in Rome. His heartfelt plea was that I would intervene with Tom to ensure that the pre-planned timetable, the one that had no reference to anything that was happening in the North, would not be disrupted. I told him that O'Gara was his own man and that I agreed with his argument and his annoyance. I am not certain of this, but I have a notion that the bishops never ran another such event. I do know for certain that the administrator was appointed a bishop a few years later.

Three years or so after the disrupted priestly conference, Tom O'Gara, who had got out of teaching and into a parish, was suspended from parish ministry by Eddie Daly and sent back to Maynooth Seminary for a study year. After Bloody Sunday and his American trip, Daly had been made head of religious broadcasting in RTÉ and then, after the death of Bishop Neil Farren in 1980, he was appointed the new bishop of Derry. He came into the job like a whirlwind. Within the first few months he visited every parish in the city for a few days and while there, visited every house in the parish that would receive him. Doors were wide open to him and there was an almost festive atmosphere. I remember standing in the Bogside, exhausted, at twelve o'clock at night, while he called to the last few houses on the street. People were delighted with his appointment, his accessibility and his pastoral outreach.

There was greater rejoicing of his appointment to bishop among the laity than there was among the priests of the diocese, from whom there was a mixed reaction. At the time and like the majority, I was initially very pleased and was expecting a new attitude and dynamic within the diocese. Some, however, thought that Daly was not academic enough for the role. I was discovering a strong academic snobbery among some priests. I lived for a short time with one who could tell me the academic placement of each priest from his class in Maynooth. I was relieved that he had no access to the academic placement of those of us educated in Rome.

Others viewed Daly as overly populist and a showman because he ran very successful concerts and pantomimes in the city. I reacted to those judgements with deserved disdain. However, Fr Tony Mulvey, who had worked with Daly in the cathedral for years, also had some reservations about his appointment to the episcopacy and I was a bit of a fan of Mulvey's. It was never explicitly expressed, but I detected it in the odd remark that he made. Mulvey was a friend of Daly's and didn't want to be seen as being jealous, in that he might have considered himself a more capable candidate. But I guessed that his biggest reservation was that Daly was too easily swayed, uncertain of his own opinions and values.

In my own short time living in the same house as Daly, I had found him enormously generous with his time and his encouragement, and was in awe of his energy, his people memory and his pastoral presence within the parish. But I had also found him emotionally reserved and underdeveloped. Conversations always stayed within the norm, within given and accepted parameters, and seldom went to the hard places. We were now in a hard place, and while I was certain that he would be an outstanding bishop on many levels, I was also sure that he would be orthodox and safe in circumstances that needed originality and risk-taking. Years later, when he became ill and stood down from the bishopric, he had the humility to say to me that he thought I was much better at politics than he was and that when I left the priesthood to get married, he was surprised that the people had much less difficulty with my leaving than he and many other clergy had.

Despite what he later said, during the worst of the Troubles, Daly never asked for my opinion or advice, and I never went to him to share any of my insights, worries or hopes. On the few occasions that people like Brendan Duddy, Martin McGuinness or others indicated a desire to share ideas or seek the support of the bishop, I always advised against it, and on the occasions when that advice wasn't taken, the feedback was that I had been correct in my advice. I don't think he ever knew, and I was guilty of not telling him, how much I would have liked to have him as a confidant and a support during some of the more difficult times, or that I thought he should have consulted me on the politics and the social issues that were dominant at the time. As the bishop, he consulted and listened to people I knew he had little respect for when he was still a priest in the parish.

My judgement wasn't based on the way Daly handled Tom O'Gara, but that would have confirmed my reservations about him. I don't recall what the issue was that led to Tom's suspension and his imposed sabbatical year back in Maynooth. I felt bad about this because I had advised Tom that he should speak to Daly, who, shortly after becoming a bishop, had announced that any priest who had a problem should come and talk to him.

The conversation between the two men clearly took a bad turn. Whatever the problem presented at that time, Tom was seen as a maverick who preached a gospel with which the local church was not fully comfortable. Within an hour of the suspension, Daly rang me, upset and nervous, explaining and justifying his decision. By that time, I was better at giving my opinion, which was that Tom had come to him to ask for advice, and that the decision to suspend him would certainly not encourage others to do the same.

Back in 1972, Tom and I were still struggling with the questions of meaning and purpose in the light of increasing hostilities on the streets. We talked of pacifism as possibly the only honest and genuine response and, if that were so, how was it to be enacted, how was it to be demonstrated? There were few people around who proclaimed themselves or might be described as pacifists. Some Quakers had come to live in the city, and they did great social, youth and prisoner-relief work, but the ones I knew were all English and lived under the mild suspicion that they had been planted by British Intelligence to keep the authorities acquainted with the mood of the community. Catholicism had neither developed nor promoted pacifism, and the anti-war movement in America, led by such people as the Berrigan brothers, was viewed by many Church authorities as anti-establishment and maverick.

I had returned from Italy in mid-1970, just as the civil rights movement was disintegrating and violence was beginning to rear its head. In my youthful idealism I had expected an extensive debate to be in progress amongst the Churches that would lead to the development of a theology that would inform a response that was pertinent to the time, to the place and to the problem. What I was confronted with were Churches traumatised by what was developing around them, thrusting them further and deeper into states of defensiveness and self-protection.

The only theology within the Catholic tradition of any substance on the use of violence was the 'just war' theory. It was thrown into the mix of the debate and arguments that were taking place within the nationalist, republican, Catholic community. Church teaching had long allowed for just wars – the use of force to stop an unjust aggression – as long as certain conditions were met. These included the exhausting of other peaceful means, the use of force that is appropriate and that won't produce worse effects, and finally that there should be a reasonable chance for success. The weakness of that teaching in Ireland and in our Troubles was that the IRA quoted it and used it as a justification for violence as often as the Church used it as a prohibitor to violence.

Tom and I met every Friday or Saturday night to try and construct a few relevant words for the Sunday Mass. I don't think what we discussed in those conversations ever got into the sermons, but the discussions were influential in forming ideas and a narrative in our own minds. Most priests and bishops, in their sermonising, when they addressed the issue at all, stuck to the line that violence was wrong. That was counteracted by press releases from the local branch of Sinn Féin or the IRA accusing the clergy of bias in condemning the violence of republicans but seldom condemning that perpetrated by the British Army and the police.

Some time after being appointed to the Long Tower parish in October 1970, I was praying over the upper torso of a body blown up in an IRA bomb. It was the remains of a young British soldier. I also cradled a young man, a child really, as death came upon his face and then his body. The bullet that killed him came from the rifle of a British soldier. I needed no one to tell me the horror of violence. What I did need was a Christian response to an ever-worsening tragedy in which most of the participants called themselves Christian. While it is true that greater tolerance and respect among the main Churches has been established between then and now, a theological and spiritual response appropriate and challenging to a society in conflict has yet to emerge.

I came to believe that the violence was an acting out of the unconscious attitudes and feelings to be found in the people who made up the conflicting groups, and one of the ways forward was to bring into consciousness and clarity the hatred, fear and distrust so dominant in the various conflicting groups – attitudes among Catholics who viewed Protestants only as unionists at prayer; among Protestants who saw Catholics as idolators; Presbyterians detesting Church of Ireland members almost as much as they detested Catholics. There was and is still much to be reconciled.

There were plenty of conscious and unconscious attitudes that needed airing amongst the Churches long before the general masses of people could be challenged. These masses had the right to, and often did, throw back the accusation that the Churches should first remove the beam from their own eyes. Reconciliation between Churches would have not only been a challenge to the politicians, it would also have created a model that the politicians and warring groups could have used, or at least found difficult to ignore.

During his banishment year in Maynooth, Tom and I put together a short treatise that captured some of the issues about priesthood that we considered important for the times and the challenges that were facing the Church and the country. Tom wrote most of it, but he generously attached my name to it. All we ever did with it was send it to a few clerical friends, but I don't remember getting much feedback. We wished to provoke a discussion, but clerics are experts at ignoring anything they don't want to engage with. It was idealistic, perhaps simplistic, but then, so is the Christian gospel.

I think our short treatise would chime well with the debate that is currently taking place within the Catholic Church. It contains some of the themes and explores some of the attitudinal and cultural changes that Pope Francis addresses in his writings and sermons – the changes that many on the conservative and traditional wing of the Church find difficult to accept. Some of the more pertinent points contained in the paper, which were valid during the years of the Troubles, certainly remain valid today, including its discussion of violence and a possible Christian response to it:

> Some of the blind spots of my ministry have been clear enough. I see a prison and men being beaten and maimed – and I wasn't with them – even when the roads were blocked off, I didn't sit down and protest. I saw truth about the political situation which my own secure position prevented me from highlighting – I have never done anything about the obvious fact that many people make fortunes from the creation of ever more powerful bombs – nor about the fact that one man makes £60,000 a year and another £4,000. Therefore, I have failed to give guidance on the important matter of justice within the fabric of society. Again, I see an ex-priest walking in solitary protest against all armies and

our ministry frowns on such protest. As a Christian I believe I am born to fight until the hour I die, but without violence. I have offered no guidance on this – no action against aggression and injustice – no line on peace for a Christian in a violent world. I have said that physical fighting is wrong – I have offered no alternative – and a protest is at least this. Had I offered an alternative some men and boys might not be dead today – perhaps I might be in prison, perhaps I would be dead. Again, I see the lack of involvement, the absence of the intertwining of peoples' lives with everlasting effect! I have felt that the young were waylaid into youth clubs and activity centres, in many cases into a mindlessness. (It is not my wish to criticise any meeting between ministers and youth and the old.) It does seem, however, that there is too much emphasis on trappings and attracting the young at the expense of the kind of relationship which pushes out a person's mind – that develops and leads a young man into concern for justice, brotherhood, love and integrity for these things.

There were also a few lines about the centrality of community. That paragraph and the idea contained in it was underdeveloped, but it touched upon something that we were discussing with each other:

I would like to pose now the most basic question that can be asked of a priest – what has he to give? Each man must answer this for himself and as he contemplates the question, he will also find himself more or less for or against what is written here. What you have to offer as a priest can only be determined after you have asked what you have to offer as a man. So many people who think they know us ask 'but what have you to offer as priests?' I make the point now that they don't know us as men – I might even ask myself if I have ever loved someone. I only know myself as an independent – as my own man. I have a fear at this point of time that I personally might be able to get by in this world without understanding within my experience love, justice, hope, hate and maybe despair. I call it fear because I wouldn't like to live a second-class life, but also because I fear to think of others who look for guidance as they ask what I have to offer. I might be able to get by, but I am proposing here that we must place ourselves, for our own sakes, and for the sake of others, in the situation where we cannot get by without sharing, without love and its suffering, without hoping and looking for justice and without prayer. And will they ask us then, 'What have you to offer as a priest?'

... I fear that as the divide between rich and poor becomes more marked, the political divisions within this community more extreme and the despair and apathy more heightened, the Church will remain trapped in holding on to her grip on the affairs of the world and she will fail to take the radical options demanded of her.

During the next ten years Tom and I grew very close. He organised for a priest friend of his to marry Mary and me in a small church in Connemara, while he acted as the witness to our marriage. That day and many other days I sensed his tension and loneliness. His love of the priesthood and his unresolved growing need to love and be loved by a woman was becoming more obvious. Before that was resolved, he died in hospital from a combination of a clot and an internal bleed. He died in the middle of the night with his mother and father, Mary and me, and Bishop Eddie Daly at his bedside. Daly, true to his amazing pastoral genius, had arrived about an hour before Tom died. At those moments it is irrelevant that someone is not so good at politics.

All this time later I sometimes dream that Tom is still alive. I think he had a prophetic heart in that he was a priest and a man who was preaching a message that is closer to the original Christian message than the corrupted one that had been concocted over the centuries. At a conference in the Vatican in 2016 hosted by the Pontifical Council for Justice and Peace, and the international Catholic peace organisation, Pax Christi, the participants bluntly rejected the Catholic Church's long-held teaching on the just war theory, saying that it too often has been used to justify violent conflict. They also said that the Church must reconsider Jesus' teachings on nonviolence. And perhaps more importantly, the delegates called upon Pope Francis to issue an encyclical letter rejecting the just war theory and reorientating Catholic teaching to developing tools and capacities for nonviolent transformation of conflicts.

Those kinds of thoughts and suggestions came too late to feed into our conflict, but Tom would have rejoiced that the Church, as in many matters, would eventually catch up, even if a little late and a little breathless.

7

A Kaleidoscope of Tragedy

AFTER BLOODY SUNDAY, THE LEVEL of violence and the number of injuries and deaths rose rapidly. The statistics tell us that the greatest number of deaths in all the years of the Troubles took place in 1972, the year following Bloody Sunday, but the deaths that impacted most on the people of the Long Tower parish and on myself were spread out over that year and the next. It was a kaleidoscope of tragedies.

It was March 1972. I was sound asleep when the call came through. I always woke with a jolt when the phone rang in the middle of the night. In the befuddled state of being abruptly awakened from a deep sleep, the priority was to get the gist of the message. The details would become clear later. On this occasion, someone had been shot and was in a house in Dove Gardens. A priest was wanted.

I owned a Mini in those days and as I drove down the hilly, narrow streets, the only illumination came from the lights of my small car because the streetlamps had been extinguished by the army. Suddenly I had to brake and pull onto the footpath to avoid a Saracen tank being driven fast up a hill with no lights except a powerful lamp being held by the soldier on the turret, who was shouting through a megaphone at me to get off the road.

By the time I reached the house a small group of neighbours had gathered, and they moved aside to allow me into the kitchen where a body was lying on the floor. I knelt beside it and began the prayers, opening the small metal container that held the oils used in Extreme Unction, the sacrament of anointing the dying. The paleness of the face and the coolness of the skin as I rubbed the oil on his forehead were nearly always signs of death.

Before I could ask any questions about what had happened, someone alerted me to the fact that there was another body outside. A few neighbours were standing around a man lying on the cold pavement – again he had that same paleness of face and cooling skin. An ambulance had been sent for, but that was only out of respect and the wish to adhere to proper procedures. There was no one there in any doubt that two young men were dead.

There had been a gun battle between the IRA and the army, which had gone on for a considerable time. I was never sure how the IRA organised themselves in those days. It appeared that a small group of volunteers patrolled the nationalist areas of the Bogside and Creggan during the night-time hours. Volunteers, of course, were mostly young men who had flocked to the cause after Bloody Sunday. The night-time hours were also when the British Army made their strongest sorties into the area, either to engage the IRA or to make arrests. Many of the soldiers in the army were young men of similar ages and backgrounds to those in the IRA, the difference being that they had longer and better training in the use of firearms.

There is a comprehensive book called *Lost Lives* that records all the killings during the Troubles, giving the names, ages and organisations, if any, of those killed. But most references and accounts of killings are not confined to the judgement-free, impartial accounts contained in *Lost Lives*. I came across the following posted online in March 2020. It was about the two deaths I was attending that night in May 1972 and must have been a commemorative notice:

> IRA volunteers Colm Keenan and Eugene McGillan were shot dead by British soldiers in the Dove Gardens area of the Bogside on March 14, 1972.
>
> Both men were unarmed when they were killed following a gun battle between the IRA and a British patrol.
>
> Colm Keenan, a son of veteran Derry republican, Sean Keenan, was described as a lieutenant in the Derry brigade of the IRA at the time of his killing.
>
> Their shootings took place on the last day of the Widgery Tribunal into the events of Bloody Sunday and it was claimed at the Saville Inquiry by a former British Army intelligence officer that a group of military lawyers joined the troops on patrol in the Bogside that night and were involved in the gun battle.
>
> Three British soldiers were also wounded during the gun battle.
>
> The two young IRA men were taken into houses in the area after they had been shot. Local residents who attempted to assist the wounded teenagers insisted that neither was armed despite claims of the British that they were.
>
> The funerals of both IRA men were held under what

was described at the time as 'one of the strictest security operations mounted in Derry since the Troubles began.'

Colm Keenan was buried with full military honours and his funeral was attended by more than 8,000 people while Eugene McGillan's funeral was private.

Sean Keenan was released from Long Kesh, where he was interned at the time, to attend his son's funeral.

Despite the increased security, which included a ring of RUC and military checkpoints being thrown up around the Bogside and Creggan, IRA Chief of Staff Seán Mac Stíofáin and leading Belfast Provisional Martin Meehan managed to get into Derry for the funeral of Colm Keenan.

Mac Stíofáin was introduced to deliver the oration by Martin Meehan, who described him as the Provisional IRA Chief of Staff.

In his oration, the IRA Chief of Staff, at the time one of the most wanted men in Ireland, paid tribute to the two Derry teenagers.

'Two more revolutionary soldiers have given their lives for their people. Just a few weeks ago 13 sons of Derry were shot dead and this week we mourn the deaths of two more. Next week, maybe next month, who knows who will be next?' he said.

He also said that only when Ireland as a whole country had peace could a proper tribute be paid to the men who died.

The day after the gun battle and the deaths of young Keenan and McGillan, a British Army officer, a captain I think, called at the parochial house asking to speak to me. It wasn't a daily occurrence, but army chaplains and majors of incoming regiments would often drop in to introduce themselves. The captain was not one of those. He had seen me around the streets and wanted to talk about the shooting and deaths in Dove Gardens the night before. He had not been in the army all that long and, while he couldn't be certain, he was almost sure that he had shot either Keenan or McGillan. It was the first time he had killed someone, and he wanted, needed, to talk about it. I listened and he talked. He was very distressed about the shooting. After an hour or so he left. I never saw him again.

Conflict, uprising, Troubles – these were a few of the descriptions of that time – but the least commonly used term was the word war. That may have been because there were no missiles or bombs falling from the skies and because the governments didn't wish to politicise the situation, but living in one of the worst-affected areas, where the violence was growing, it was beginning to feel like a war, especially after the next death in the parish.

It was late evening, and I was visiting in a house right beside the Brandywell football stadium when the explosion happened. By this juncture in the Troubles most people were used to the distinctive noises of guns, pipe bombs, nail bombs and explosions, and most had become expert at knowing the likely distance and thus the likely district in which an explosion occurred.

This was different. There was no distance to be gauged on this one, it was right in our midst. Houses shook and panes of glass shattered onto the pavements. After the few minutes needed to recover from the immediate shock, the locals, including myself, flocked onto the streets. There was the usual chatter and huddling together, enquiring as to where it had happened. It was not many minutes before a woman approached me saying, 'Father, I think there is a body in our backyard.'

Behind the two-up two-down terrace houses, there was a laneway running parallel. There were several sheds and outhouses: Paddy Melaugh, a well-known local man reared pigs in one of the sheds. He collected brock – discarded food – from the houses and businesses in the area to feed his pigs, which were housed in one of the outhouses.

I went with the woman and entered the backyard through her small kitchen. It was dark. It took a few seconds to adjust to the darkness and to identify what looked like a body, except it wasn't a full body. I hesitated, wondering if it might be an animal rather than a person. But when I knelt beside the torso there was no doubt that it was that of a man, blown up and partly disjointed by the power of the blast. It was impossible to know if he was a soldier, an IRA man, a local who had been working in one of the outhouses or just a passer-by who had been walking in the narrow laneway. I mumbled the prayers of the dying and made the sign of the cross on the back of the body with the oils of anointing. It was a small yard surrounded by a brick wall and the shouts of the army as they nervously moved in and around the laneway.

I don't remember much of the following hour. I presume the army took away the body. People were reporting that the bomb had been planted in a shed and the bomb squad had tried to defuse it, but it had exploded, killing at least one soldier. *Lost Lives* had not yet been published, so in the coming years I did not know the name of the dead soldier whom I had prayed over. I always regretted that I didn't contact the army chaplain, or he me, so I could learn the name and history of this man. I did not find out if he had a family who may or may not have wanted to talk about the manner of his death, although I presume the army would have informed his family of the details. I could not have added much, but it struck me, years later, that if the person killed had not been a soldier, I would have made greater efforts to find out about him and his family and enquired if they wished to know that I had been there shortly after he had died.

In the National Memorial Arboretum in Burton upon Trent in England there is a statue of a soldier in a bomb-disposal outfit with the names of all the soldiers from that unit killed in the Troubles. One of the names inscribed is that of Captain Barry Stanley Gritten. According to online information, Captain Gritten was a member of the Royal Army Ordnance Corps who was '[k]illed in the early hours of the 21st June 1973 by explosion whilst clearing a bomb making factory in a Nissen hut near the Lecky Road, Londonderry, Northern Ireland. Born 16th January 1944 and died aged 29. His remains were cremated, and his ashes scattered on the grounds of Welbeck College, Loughborough, Leicester.'

Shortly after anointing what I now know was Captain Gritten's body, I was approached again and asked to go to a nearby house to talk to a young man who was in distress. I didn't know him as he was not from the parish. He spoke very quietly and hesitantly and told me that he had set the bomb. He had made bombs before, he continued, but he didn't think they had killed anyone. I sat with him for an hour, talked and drank a cup of tea. He was very shocked and emotional, but then so was I. I have no memory of what we talked about; I think there were long silences when we just sat and said nothing. There was too much to be said and neither of us was in any shape to say it. He didn't tell me his name and I didn't ask him. I think we ran across each other on one or two occasions in the following years, but I couldn't swear to that. He never came back to talk about it again. If I have got the right person in my head, he died years ago. But I am not certain of that either.

The next day I announced from the altar that I was organising a meeting in the local church hall that evening to talk about the events and the killing of the night before. There was a deep need in me to say something public, but there was always a reluctance to use the pulpit as a political platform. Where politics ends and the existential begins is always a dilemma. I was as conscious and as careful about that as the next priest, but I would have felt contaminated and cowardly to have ignored the brutal killing that had happened a few hundred yards from the church building. The compromise was to use the altar to call for a meeting in the church hall, inviting everyone from the parish who wanted to attend. I asked Fr Tom O'Gara to come with me for support.

About sixty people turned up at the small hall. Tom began the meeting with a few words about violence and the way it was addressed in the Christian scriptures. I spoke of my experience and my deep shock and sorrow over what had happened the night before. Not very eloquently, I talked of understanding the frustration and the complexity of the political situation but called upon people to reject violence. Before I could finish speaking, a man came into the hall saying quite loudly that he had just come from Creggan, the neighbouring parish, and that the army was raiding houses and arresting people. The mood of the small gathering changed.

I didn't think that the 'Creggan raids' man had attended the meeting of his own accord. He arrived late and was quite prepared to interrupt the meeting. *You have been sent,* I thought to myself. Even in the middle of disruption and in the face of death, the propaganda battle between the combatants was alive and active. He was only a cog in a much bigger wheel. Over the years I used to see him at meetings and social events. He was probably a good-enough man, but I could never warm to him. I wasn't without my own prejudices.

I suppose that meeting was a marker, in that it didn't allow the terrible death of a young man whose name we didn't even know at the time to go without some acknowledgement, but in the wider context of what was happening, it was inconsequential. It left me very flat and pondering the age-old dilemma of whether to accept or try to change reality, while understanding that pride and ego can be as great a motivator as compassion or love.

I was getting to know myself somewhat better. I was becoming a more public person in the public square, and I liked it. I was less of the shy little boy who hid under the table when his schoolteacher visited his home and more one who was confident and willing to give his opinion to the nearest journalist. I hadn't lost my decorum nor fully overcome my innate shyness, but I was now more conscious of my ego and of its strength in the initiation and motivation of my actions. I wasn't silly enough to think that anyone can be fully free of ego, but I often compared myself unfavourably to my father, who seemed to be as free of it as a human being can be.

When I went to confession, I would often confess that the purity of my motivation left much to be desired. I even delivered a sermon about St Paul describing a thorn in his side, which was mostly interpreted as him having sexual temptations. I proposed in the sermon that the thorn was not sexual temptation but egotism. I was becoming fearful that I would end up as a good professional priest, who would be present for and offer comfort to people in their sorrow-filled moments but would never love anyone enough to experience the full pain of loss. But in those days and in that place, there was only a very short time and space for reflection before the next tragic event intervened.

I wasn't there the night that Seamus Brown was executed by the IRA. But the Sunday after his death I did something that was not all that common. I didn't call a meeting in the church hall this time. I used the sermon at Mass to talk about Seamus, about how evil and wrong it was to kill someone like him. It was somewhat unusual for a priest to home in on one specific killing, using the person's name and the circumstances of his death. There were many sermons on violence and killings, but they were more likely to be generalised or contained within a funeral service. There was always a tension about using the pulpit as a political bandstand, but I was too angry and annoyed on this occasion to be concerned with theological niceties.

I have no recollection of what exactly I said from the pulpit, but what I wanted to say is best captured in an article I wrote years later. As the Troubles began to move away from violence and into the political arena, I was writing a fortnightly column in *The Irish News*. I had been sent a poem and a letter from America, remembering Seamus' killing, which put me in a dilemma. I knew that if I wrote from my heart and included the poem, it would more than likely hurt Seamus' family, but if I asked their permission, they would probably refuse to give it. So I talked it over with a few people and eventually decided I would write without asking Seamus' sister, who I knew was still living in Derry. The article reads:

Seamus Brown should not have died. Seamus Brown should not have been executed. His death has haunted me for almost thirty years. Of all the deaths I witnessed and experienced during all the years of the Troubles, the death of Seamus Brown is the one that turned me most against violence and against war. More than any other, his death taught me that war is a dirty and ruthless thing and that there is no manner of fighting and killing that is not dirty and ruthless and hard. That dirt and that ruthlessness and that hardness rubs off on all of us who are part of it or who are caught up in it. His death taught me that to fight a war or engage in sustained and effective violence demands compromises and judgements that make us less human than we should be.

Seamus Brown did not have a very easy life. He grew up amidst hardship and poverty. He was not very bright at school and would probably be considered in these enlightened days to be in need of special tuition. He walked with a funny little trot, and he had acquired some but not all of the street craft that was common to the times and the conditions.

I liked him. I think he liked me. He could be and often was a bit of a 'torture', but he possessed enough roguishness to make the 'torture' acceptable. I was more than happy to be the priest that married him and his wife, Mary.

The Provos claimed that he was 'touting' for the Brits and the police and that was the reason they shot him. He might well have been' touting' but the evidence produced was very flimsy and if Seamus had information that was worth a 'tuppeny curse' to anyone then shame on those who let him have the information. But that was not the reason Seamus Brown died. He died for the 'expediency' of war.

The Brits and the police had no access to the republican/nationalist heartlands, so any source of information was welcome and expendable. That is part of the 'expediency' of war. The Provos arose from a community that was mostly economically poor and often given to gossip. Money and flattery were a threat to the war effort, so Seamus Brown had to be executed as an example to others. That is part of the 'expediency' of war.

I was relieved and somewhat consoled when I discovered recently that it is not only myself who has been haunted by his death. In a poem written by a contemporary and a long time committed republican, Seamus Brown's execution is remembered and reflected upon. In the poem Seamus's executioner speaks the lines:

I will not look at his eyes – kind eyes, stupid eyes,
soon to be dead eyes.
I heft the implement, secrete it with my doubts and guilt
As they say, 'He'll soon be kilt'
And I, what of me – amnesia from the drink
Will I die a little too?
Of course he's guilty – no questions there, but he's stupid,
And poor and small of stature, and maybe doesn't smell
Good at times. Which thing do I kill him for?'

I finished off the article by addressing the IRA's reluctance to decommission their weapons. I wrote that it would be a step they would not wish to take but that they should take it for the 'expediency' of peace and politics, and that it would also be a small but significant atonement for all the Seamus Browns whose lives were forfeited for the 'expediency' of war.

A few days after the article was published, I received a phone call from Seamus' sister. She was very angry with me for writing the article and said that the least I should have done was to ask her permission. I asked if I could call at her home to talk face to face, which I did the next day. Despite the appearance that I often gave in public, I was no good at confrontation, especially if I thought I had hurt someone. It was an enormous relief when I arrived at the house to be told by Seamus' sister that she and her husband had talked and thought about it and that she had changed her mind. She was now glad that I had written the article. It was right, she said, to publicly state how awful and how unjust it was to kill Seamus Brown.

Billy McGreanery had been killed at the junction of Westland Street with the Lone Moor Road. Captain Barry Gritten was killed at the sheds at the back of the Lecky Road. Seamus Brown was killed somewhere along the River Foyle, at the end of the Lecky Road. Those three locations were within a quarter mile of each other. Those were three adult murders.

Kathleen Feeney was a child. She was killed crossing the Lecky Road, about fifty yards from her home and no more than a quarter of a mile from the other three deaths. She was fourteen years old. The local IRA issued a statement claiming that Kathleen had been killed by the British Army and, in retaliation, they had killed a

British soldier. The IRA took pride in the fact that, unlike the British and the RUC, it told the truth, even if the story reflected badly on it. That claim was mostly true, but not in Kathleen's case. A lie was told about her death and the death of the soldier. But because the IRA mostly took responsibility for their actions, their denial of responsibility and the claim that the British Army was trying to arouse anti-IRA sentiments in the local area would have been widely believed.

In the introduction to a book he wrote about Kathleen's death, *The Day Time Stood Still*, her brother Harry said:

> There were many different stories of how my sister Kathleen was murdered; the number of gunmen, how many shots were fired and from what location. On her thirtieth anniversary in 2003, I sat and listened to yet another version of her death. So, I decided once and for all to cut through all these ambiguities and find out what really did happen on the evening of Wednesday the 14th November 1973. Kathleen was shot dead aged fourteen years old.
>
> After the post-mortem it became evidently clear who shot her. The dogs in the street even knew who shot her, but the IRA vehemently denied that they were responsible.
>
> This story will tell how our family maintained a dignified approach yet brought the IRA to a point where they admitted and apologised for Kathleen's death. The first public apology the IRA has ever made.

I knew Kathleen because she was a regular at the parochial youth club. In the foreword to her brother's book, I described her as a feisty child and said that in Derry-speak 'you would be dying about her'. On the night of 14 November 1973 she was on her way to the youth club. There was a British Army foot patrol in the area, a regular occurrence. Kathleen began crossing the road to meet up with one of her friends, who was also going to the youth club. A shot rang out and Kathleen fell to the ground, dying.

Normally the killing of a child would have brought everything to a standstill, and for a few days that did happen. But by November 1973 the Troubles had reached such a pitch that the initial shock and anger was soon hurled, tornado-like, into the next tragedy. However, her family didn't forget. And they didn't let the IRA or Sinn Féin forget. In their quiet and dignified way, they confronted the lies that the IRA had spread at the time of Kathleen's killing. Thirty-two years later, in June 2005, the IRA released a statement saying that a review of Kathleen's death had been carried out. It said that Kathleen was hit by one of a number of shots fired by an IRA active service unit. It apologised to the Feeney family for what had happened and for all the grief caused to them by the active service unit. But as I said in the introduction to her brother's book:

> [The] hurts are most raw when your child or sister has been killed before she has had a chance to grow into the beautiful and determined young woman revealed in her childhood. It is even more hurtful when lies are told about how she was killed and who killed her. And the ultimate insult is when her death is used as an excuse to kill outsiders when the truth is that she was killed by people from her own community.
>
> In the debate about reconciliation, it is inevitable that the emphasis will be on the healing between former combatants

and former enemies. The British Army, the IRA, the RUC, UVF, UDA, etc., will capture the headlines and demand most attention. There has been less attention paid to the hurt and divisions that existed within communities. Those hurts are as real, as painful and as in need of healing as any other. Those, mostly working-class communities, had to endure for many years the presence of their 'own paramilitaries' and at the same time absorb the concentration of heavy military and police presence. Those presences over the years became more and more oppressive.

The deaths detailed here were just five from the litany of killings that took place within a short time span and within the same small neighbourhood. Two of the victims were shot by the British Army, the others were killed by the IRA. Some were combatants, one a so-called informer, the other a child who received an apology from one of the two main killing machines years after her death. This small area, this small parish to which I was attached was a snapshot, a reflection of the spiralling violence and the political vacuum that was the 1970s' Troubles. Violence now dominated everything. Those of us who lived in the Long Tower and similar areas knew that life had changed. What we didn't know was just how long that change would last.

8

The Bogside Association

'YOU WILL BE RESPONSIBLE FOR burning down Derry.' That was a bit of a jolt, especially coming from a highly respected and experienced businessman who was a bigwig in the local political world. It was not a very auspicious start to my social-action efforts. It is one thing to read and be inspired by what is contained in a book about others' lives and efforts, another to feel the corporate resistance of people or institutions. I was being told that the latest idea attached to my name was irresponsible and dangerous. If I was to push ahead with it and ignore the advice that I was now being given, I would be responsible for doing damage to the infrastructure of the city. Heady stuff.

The idea to which my name was attached was an election in the Bogside to establish an organisation that would be a substitute or replacement for the political institutions that had become dormant or were in suspension because of the growing violence and disruption. The criticism was not coming from some bystander with a passing interest in politics. The person warning me was the chairman of one of the branches of the recently formed SDLP.

Michael Canavan was an important political and business figure in Derry. I think he may also have been John Hume's election agent. He had asked to meet with me regarding an announcement in the media that I and a small number of local teachers were arranging an election in the Bogside to establish an organisation that would reflect and respond to the reality that Derry City Council had been abolished in 1969 after being accused by the civil rights movement of gerrymandering local elections. The council had been replaced by the British government with an unelected commission with no local councillors sitting on it. This meant that local political representation was no longer extant at a time when the area was embroiled in an all-out violent conflict. I thought the idea of an elected local community organisation was eminently sensible but had not yet realised that everything is political and what might seem an innocent idea could be seen by others as politically threatening.

I was not well known at this time outside the parish itself. There had been a small amount of publicity about a hostel for street drinkers that I had established, which had been a reactive response rather than a pre-planned strategy. On a foggy November evening in 1972, I was driving back from visiting my mother and father, and was scheduled to say the 7.30 p.m. Mass. On a street close to the church, I almost ran over a man who was lying in the middle of the street. He was very drunk and what was described in those days as a 'skid-row' alcoholic. Gun battles had become more common and while lying in the street is never a good idea at any time, it was particularly dangerous in those years. I got him into the back seat of the car; after Mass he was still sound asleep, if somewhat warmer. There was a Simon Community in another area of the city, but it was not in the location where the skid-row drinkers congregated. On that night I got him a bed in the Simon hostel, but I knew he would be back in the Bogside the next morning and began thinking of a solution.

I started looking for somewhere in the parish that would be suitable for such cases to stay. I knew of a row of small terrace houses, some of them falling into disrepair, others occupied and the rest recently vacated, as people were moving on to other parts of the city where new houses were being built and where the Troubles were less intrusive. Mrs Kelly, one of the residents, was about to move out, and when I told her that I was trying to get a house where the drinkers could sleep overnight, she told me she would be delighted if her home, where she was born and reared, would be used for that purpose. She would even leave bits of furniture and cutlery and make sure that the place was tidy and clean.

The street was called St Columb's Wells and so the hostel became known, for want of a better name, as the House in the Wells. Initially it provided beds and meals for about ten men. It was staffed and managed by volunteers until it developed into a much larger facility for a greater number of men with paid staff. During the first three or four years all essential supplies, such as meat, bread, milk and coal, were supplied to the hostel by small local businesses. It took up very little of my time because all the work was done by a group of men and women from the parish.

A few years later, the founder of the Simon Community, Anton Wallich-Clifford, came to see the House. He had been a probation officer in London and encountered many street drinkers. He initially established a farm outside London where people could go for a change and a rest. That led to hostels in some of the larger urban centres in England. Anton had also been influenced by the work of Dorothy Day in America.

He loved the ambience and the community/parish rootedness of the House in the Wells. He came back a few times and always insisted on sleeping in the House itself. It is good to be able to say that fifty years later the House has evolved into a very professional organisation and, while the volunteerism has disappeared, it still serves a cohort of street drinkers and is still warmly supported by the local community.

The acceptance of that initiative by the community and the fact that the ownership of the project was taken up by local people and local businesses gave me some confidence that my interests and judgements were not completely awry. So, when I ran into heavy criticism and opposition to setting up, by election, an organisation that would have a presence and a voice in the social life of the community, I had some experience from which to draw. But I didn't fully appreciate the reaction the new initiative would generate among those who were vying for political authority.

Before the election even took place, the tussle for support and political authority between republicans and the recently formed SDLP came to the fore, with me in the middle of it. The ramifications of Bloody Sunday were still playing out. The demand for civil rights, supported by the SDLP and tolerated by the British government but denied by Stormont, was now competing with a rising vocal and violent demand, supported by the IRA, for an end to Stormont and a withdrawal of British rule from Ireland.

In Derry, we were at a state where we had no local councillors and were in something of a political vacuum. At this time the old Nationalist Party was being replaced by the SDLP. John Hume

had defeated Eddie McAteer and Eamonn McCann in an election
to Stormont in 1969, but the SDLP, founded the following year,
was still trying to bring disparate politicians together as a cohesive
party. The IRA had been energised by the repercussions of Bloody
Sunday but was struggling to respond to the increased demand for
membership from the young. Too many immature and unvetted
youngsters were as great a danger to the organisation as too few.
It had already become confident of the authority that came from
the gun, and that was now being enhanced by growing support
from a great number of the people who lived in working-class
areas of the North. The Bogside, the Long Tower parish was one
of those areas. Violence had become the dominant factor in life,
and everything was subservient to that.

The local IRA was well advanced in bombing the heart out of
Derry city, but it is interesting that one of the articles in the pages
of the *Derry Journal*, the main organ for news in Derry in those
days, described the prospect of the Provisional IRA organising
a local election to an, as yet, undefined body. The article was
headed 'Provos' Election Plan Opposed' and read:

> In a statement last night Derry Citizens Central Council
> said, 'In competition with the proposed Provisional IRA
> election, the Council does not consider that there is a
> united and authoritative view on the framework of such an
> election, particularly as the elected representative has not
> been consulted.'
>
> It is understood that the Council feel that the elected
> representatives of the people are the only ones with the right
> to decide whether such elections should be held and when
> they should be held. And at the moment, due to the absence

of any Corporation or other elected local Government body, Mr John Hume, as the only elected representative, should have the right to make such decisions on behalf of the people who elected him.

I don't know now who or what the Derry Citizens Central Council was, but it is clear from the article that it was more than just me who had recognised the existence of a political vacuum. As an aside, it is interesting that the *Derry Journal* article does not use the words Sinn Féin. In those years, few if any referenced Sinn Féin. That would come later; in those days it was the 'boys' or the 'Provos'.

I had innocently, probably naively, stumbled into a situation fuelled by political tension and rivalry. I don't know if I was operating out of arrogance, innocence, insight or instinct, or a mixture of all of those, but it shocks me to realise that I had only been in the parish for about eighteen months when I fronted the setting up of an organisation that was judged a challenge to the both the primary nationalist political party and to the IRA. At the time I quickly began to understand why the SDLP were annoyed with me and to realise that the Provos were thinking of dipping their toe into local politics.

I had been talking with local teachers, mostly Eamon Deane, who taught in the local primary school and who was highly regarded and admired by his pupils, many of whom were now putting themselves forward for admittance to the IRA. It was Eamon who did most of the preparatory work for our proposed organisation. He and I had gone to Dublin to visit a community group in Ballyfermot, set up with the help of Ivor Brown, a well-known psychiatrist, and Paddy Wally, an economist, under a foundation that they had established. They were exploring and implementing ideas in local communities, organising themselves to have an influence in local affairs. It was a combination of economic and mental health and well-being for the residents of working-class communities who were feeling marginalised and neglected. Importantly, they promised us seed money if we decided to establish a community group.

Given my interest and reading around the ideas of Chavez, Alinsky, the Berrigans and others, I was convinced there was a need for a structure within the community that gave some voice to local people and local needs. In the absence of local councillors, and amid increasing killing and death, it was going to be so easy to crush the spirit of the people even further. Not that I should give the impression that everyone felt crushed. There were many who felt liberated and exulted in what was happening on the streets. A large number believed they were part of the 'risen people', off their knees for the first time in their lives. But if there were many of those, there was an equal number who felt the oppression of violence from all sides and were fearful and intimidated by the killing, the maiming and the paramilitary and military presence on their streets.

It soon became clear that the local IRA were ambiguous about this idea of an elected community organisation. While they were antagonistic to anything that challenged their growing authority and leadership of the local community, idealistically they could not be seen to be negative to the voice of the people. Some feedback I received alerted me to the fact that they would not oppose the election for the association and would not proceed with their own proposed election, but that they would try to get a few of their own people into it.

What I wasn't ready for was being told that I would be responsible for the burning of Derry. It was my first real clash with the hard edge of party politics. I remember thinking that I was only a young cub pitted against someone who was much older and more experienced in politics and the ways of the world. I argued the case that the people of the area were without local representation and needed a local mechanism to interject between the tugs and tensions that were now part of their everyday experience. The setting up of a new political party like the SDLP and the movement of the leadership of the civil rights into that party had its own rationality and integrity but would not, initially at least, serve the needs of a locality like the Bogside. I made arguments that I thought were valid and persuasive, while feeling a determination to resist the pressure and bullying that I was experiencing.

I failed to convince Canavan of the attractiveness of a local community association, but underneath the shock of being told that I would be responsible for burning Derry, I was aware of my own even greater determination to push ahead with the idea. So, on a pleasant Sunday in April 1972, the election for the Bogside Community Association took place. It was organised on a version of the French model. Two elections were held, the first entailing the nomination of people in a designated area, whose names were then put on a ballot paper for the second election, which took place a week later. It was a cumbersome but fair and interesting exercise in democracy in a turbulent time.

By Monday night the votes had been counted. The *Derry Journal* announced:

The Bogside Community Association on Sunday met the people who organised and supervised the election of the twelve-man committee and afterwards a statement made it clear that the Association would undertake the task laid down by the organisers in their original statement of aims, namely to improve the recreational facilities and amenities, to improve the social environment and to discourage vandalism and crime in the area.

The announcement after Sunday's meeting also made it clear that some of the elected members of the Association had reservations about the method and form of the election.

It said, 'The BCA itself recognises the limitations of the method of the election but will remain in being and attempt to serve the interests of the people of the Bogside.'

As a first step the BCA calls upon everyone in the area to interest themselves in the workings of the tenants' associations, youth organisations and other social bodies.

The BCA planned to meet last night to draw up a constitution and general set of rules under which it will operate. It will also have to co-opt seven [*sic*] members as requested by the organisers as the plan for the Association. The attitude of Mr. John Hume M.P. is not known. He stated before the election that he was opposed to it in principle. Mr. Hume is in America but is expected home today. He was one of those elected to the Association in the election in which about 4,500 of the 6,000 Bogsiders over eighteen entitled to vote exercised their franchise.

This statement concluded with a list of those appointed. Twelve men from across the area known as the Bogside were elected to serve on the association. Those twelve in turn had the responsibility, under the terms of the election, to appoint eight more people to the association itself, to ensure a greater representativeness. Significantly, no women had been elected, but the appointments slightly rectified that imbalance. Although John Hume was elected to a seat, he never took it up. There were at least two members of the old Nationalist Party elected and two who were very close to Sinn Féin, even if they were not card-carrying members.

In another page of the same *Journal* there were articles that reveal the atmosphere and the tensions of the times in which the organisation was coming into existence. Under the headline 'Bombed Derry City Centre Premises' was recorded:

> The Provisional IRA in Derry yesterday defeated the anti-bombing security precautions in the city centre and planted a bomb which extensively damaged the premises of McConnell and Co. tea merchants, in Foyle Street. Two men drove a van, which had been hijacked a short time before in William Street, into the enclosed yard of McConnell's premises and left it, saying they would be back in a few minutes. The area was evacuated a half-hour before the bomb went off. The enclosed yard sent the blast upwards, thus minimising the effect.

The same article goes on to report: 'Violence broke out in William Street as crowds of youths threw stones at troops. The youths also attacked an army Saracen in Little James St. Some of the youths had sticks and shields.'

A week or so after the election, Ivor Brown came to Derry and I introduced him to Paddy 'Bogside' Doherty, who had been one of the local leaders of the civil rights movement. It was obvious that the embryonic Bogside Community Association would need a manager. Ivor agreed that his organisation would pay a manager's wages until we found another source of income, and I persuaded the association that this was an acceptable arrangement to get the association up and running. Paddy had been in Jamaica for about eighteen months working on a large building project for the McAlpine company and had only recently returned to the city. He agreed to take the job on a temporary basis and the association agreed that, in the circumstances, there was no need for an interview.

Paddy was best known as the 'king of the Bogside'. He had been the most prominent face and voice during the years of 'Free Derry', when the area was barricaded off, the army and police were forbidden entrance, and the 'battle of the Bogside', as it was called, took place. He had a strong, even forceful personality. He had a reputation within the building industry as a very capable foreman. He brought those skills to the Bogside Association, setting up an office which became the focal point and the centre of mediation for the interactions of the residents with the army, the IRA and the various local authorities that were still operating.

The association involved itself in planning and building some houses for pensioners. It organised sporting events for the youth of the area and it encouraged some of the small businesses to co-operate in buying a former shirt factory, which was then turned into a job-training centre. But everything was subject to events and the area was a cauldron of events. The British government had had enough of 'Free Derry' and its connotations.

In the early hours of 31 July 1972, what was called 'Operation Motorman' began – an attempt by the British Army to retake so-called no-go areas in both Derry and Belfast. That morning,

Paddy Doherty and I were walking the streets of the Bogside. There had been no resistance because the entry of the army had been well signalled in advance and the IRA was not arrogant or stupid enough to test themselves against what was described as the biggest movement of troops and armour on these islands since the Second World War. It was eerie walking streets deserted of people but with tanks commanding every corner. The only time any of us had seen anything similar was when the Soviet Union invaded Czechoslovakia – but that was a TV event.

At one of those intersections sat a solitary ambulance. No paramedics or driver were to be seen. There were soldiers in the vicinity showing little interest in the ambulance when Paddy and I arrived. A man standing in his doorway said to me that he thought there might be bodies in it. There were two, one on each of the trolley beds, covered with the familiar NHS blankets – two young men, not yet in their twenties. I was experienced enough by then to know they had been dead for some time. I anointed both with the oils that priests carry and said a few prayers. I asked the man at the door if he had any idea who either of the young men were, but he just shook his head.

It would be later that day before it became clear that Seamus Bradley and Daniel Hegarty were both shot by the army in Creggan, the neighbouring parish. The official version was of a gun battle in which the two young boys were shot dead. Decades elapsed before that official version was overturned and the story told of two innocent boys shot dead in the tension and mayhem of politics and violence.

Motorman, this military smashing of symbolic separation, was taking place in the middle of summertime. This was the busy time for weddings. I had been booked to officiate at three weddings on the morning of the operation, one at eight o'clock, one at ten and one at twelve. It was getting close to eight as I stepped out of the ambulance. Someone else would have to see to the dead on this morning. Going between the church and the street, the brides and grooms and the soldiers, between the living and the dead, I had to grow up and learn fast. And I had no need to make any excuses on that day as to why I couldn't attend the wedding receptions.

British Army, Provisional IRA, a small residual Official IRA and the people of the parish were now interacting cheek by jowl. The Troubles were becoming more complex, more tense, more violent and more dominant in all our lives. I was more convinced than ever that an organisation was needed that had a modicum of authority and some capacity to intervene, when possible, in the plethora of problems that played out daily. But it was clear by this stage that community development and social action was a finger in a dam that was already gushing a torrent of water with the potential to create havoc and take a lot of lives.

Some of us were being forced to think beyond the social, beyond the local, to where the core of the Troubles lay and, hopefully, to where a resolution and solution lay. The Bogside Association made a few small stabs in that direction. Willie Whitelaw, the then Secretary of State for Northern Ireland, came into the area and had a long meeting with the association. I was present but mostly quiet. It was my first meeting with a senior British politician. He was likeable and anxious to please. But the conversation largely stayed on the safe ground of social and economic conditions, sometimes straying into the more contentious issue of British Army behaviour on the streets.

I think the association got some kudos out of this meeting and it certainly improved our status in dealing with statutory bodies, but it was all a million miles from the core of the problem. An association was clearly not the vehicle for addressing what had morphed into the continuation of the historical Anglo-Irish problem.

The Ulster Workers' strike took place in the early days of the association, between 15 and 28 May 1974. The strike was by unionists who were against the Sunningdale Agreement, which had been signed in December 1973 and was an attempt to establish a power-sharing executive in Northern Ireland and a cross-border Council of Ireland. Specifically, the strikers opposed the sharing of political power with Irish nationalists and the proposed role for the Republic of Ireland's government in running Northern Ireland.

As a result of that strike, the local gas company was not getting a supply of chemicals that was used in manufacturing its product. Many of the houses in the area used gas as their main source of energy. It was the same gas yard where Phil Coulter claimed his school played ball and laughed through the smoke and the smell in his song 'The Town I Loved so Well'. The association was told that the chemicals were available in Dublin, but we couldn't get a precise answer if, in light of the strike, the suppliers in Dublin would be prepared to sell to the Derry company. Someone suggested that we should go to Dublin in person, rather than be subject to imprecise messages on the phone.

Six of us set out early one morning and drove to Dundalk, where we bought an old oil tanker. It was on the proviso that we would get our money back if we failed to get the chemicals and the need for the tanker was redundant. I was the only one who had a cheque book, so it was my signature on the cheque. I wouldn't have thought that there was that amount of money in my account.

We arrived in Dublin and parked the tanker close to the Shelbourne Hotel. Within minutes the gardaí arrived. Explanations were given and phone calls made. It wasn't that long before we were escorted to a government department where we met a government minister. He was gracious and promised that he would get his officials to enquire about the chemicals used in the production of gas in the Dublin area. We hung around for a few hours before receiving a call from the government department to say that, after enquiries, the chemicals in Dublin and Derry were not compatible. Back to Dundalk and the return of my cheque.

Months later I was told that the information we were given was incorrect and that the chemicals were the same. Sometimes it was difficult to know who or what to believe. Thankfully, the Ulster Worker's Strike came to an end before we ran out of gas in Derry.

In between Troubles' incidents, the Bogside Association organised events, sports and outings for the elderly and the youth. One of the lesser but memorable things it did was erect a Christmas crib. It was built in the heart of the Bogside, along one of the gas-yard walls. It was well lit and in the darkness of the December nights it had an ambience and a serenity that was added to when the IRA called a ceasefire for a few days over the Christmas period.

The association liaised and argued with the army and the police when families sought information on their arrested sons or daughters. It talked and often argued with the local leaders of the IRA. It served a purpose for four or five years until it morphed into a larger organisation called the Inner-City Trust, which endeavoured to transform Derry city within the walls, buying and renovating property and establishing a training facility for young adults. That organisation is still extant and doing excellent restoration and organising innovative schemes.

The Bogside Association did some good work and filled a gap that needed attention. It was an interesting project in the circumstances of the time but was naturally restricted in its ambitions by the violence that dominated the area and the whole of the North. While it never became the transformative vehicle that some of us would have wished it to be, neither did it contribute to the burning of Derry, and, in a small way, it may have prevented some fires from ever being lit.

9

The Backchannel

IT WAS IRONIC BUT MAYBE fitting that the initial promptings for a backchannel, a link between the IRA and the British government came from the local superintendent of the RUC, Frank Lagan. He had strong views that would not have been considered mainstream within the ranks of policing or the politics of the time and had little tolerance for the analysis that the events happening on the streets were a little local difficulty orchestrated by a group of criminals. He was clear that we were again living through the old tensions and unresolved divisions between Anglo and Irish streams of history.

Astute to the impossibility of resolving the situation merely through military power and might, Lagan was a policeman with influence trying to hold a maelstrom of issues in a perspective that would provide as much safety to the community as possible, while, at the same time, facing an increasing breakdown of law and order. I think he knew that his localised efforts had been destroyed by the actions of the Parachute Regiment on Bloody Sunday and that the only positive move left to him was to convince MI6 that they should persuade their political masters to engage with the IRA to find a settlement.

The lines and the sequencing between the British and the IRA were not always as linear as is described in articles and books dealing with the Troubles. Underneath the contacts and the developments, the personalities and the quirks and wrinkles in the relationships may have been as influential as the events themselves.

I had first got to know Brendan Duddy when the House in the Wells, the hostel for street drinkers, was set up. Duddy owned a fish-and-chip shop in William Street and was acutely aware of the issues I had begun to observe around the street drinkers. Many of the skid-row drinkers frequented Duddy's chip shop, especially around closing time, and it was impossible not to worry for their well-being after the shop closed, with their nearest refuge, the Simon Community hostel, miles away in another part of the city. Before I helped set up the House in the Wells, I talked to Duddy. He was very supportive and encouraging that such a project should happen.

Duddy and John Hume had been reared in the same area of the city. Both had attended St Columb's College, but Duddy left early and never went on to third-level education or a profession. Although he hid it well and succeeded in business, he was always conscious of what he considered his educational deficit. I think he always felt himself to be in the shadow of Hume, and on at least one occasion they had a rip-roaring row about the politics of the civil rights movement and the direction that politics in the nationalist community should take in the future.

My relationship with Noel Gallagher evolved in a normal-enough fashion, in that he lived and had a business in the heart of the Brandywell, right in the centre of the parish where I worked. Born and reared in the Bogside, Gallagher and Martin McGuinness grew up together and Gallagher would claim that Martin was half-reared in his house. Gallagher's parents were dead before I got to know him, but there was a wonderfully rich entrepreneurial and idiosyncratic quality in the extended family and Gallagher inherited a fair dose of it. The son of a cattle dealer and small-time entrepreneur, by the time I got to know him, horses and coal were the mainstay of his business. He had at one time been a national organiser of Sinn Féin – a grand title for a position in a political party that at the beginning of the century had been substantial in its membership and influential in the affairs of Irish republicanism, but which had dissipated and shrivelled over the decades. During Gallagher's tenure, the party had little profile apart from the fact that its president, Ruairí Ó Brádaigh, was someone to whom the Army Council looked for a political steer.

As well as owning a small coal business, Gallagher bought and sold horses all over Ireland, England and Scotland. He knew every corner of Northern Ireland and had a good grasp of the rest of Ireland. In addition to knowing small farmers and horsey people throughout the length of these islands, he had a unique understanding of republicans, which he used to great effect in the long and torturous journey from violence to politics. He is always referred to as the third person of the backchannel, but in some ways, he was the most important. The negotiations between the IRA and the British were vital, but only ever became transformative when they morphed into a pan-nationalist coalition that was followed by Anglo-Irish negotiations. Gallagher would go on to become an important stanchion in the bridge that facilitated that journey and supported that transformation.

McGuinness, Gallagher and I had come to know each other around the normal parish events as well as the troubles on the streets, but I think that grew closer to friendship when and because of an event involving the two women who were to become their wives. The army stopped a car of an evening and Berni and Marie, the driver and passenger, were arrested and charged with transporting material that would be helpful to terrorists. They were in their teens at the time. I was friendly with both their families. When they appeared in court a few days later, Tom O'Gara and I went bail for them to the tune of £1000: a lot of money in the early 1970s. We would have found it difficult to scrape a few hundred pounds together, but we were certain that the families would not allow their daughters to abscond and leave the poor young priests in the lurch. When the trial was held, Berni, Martin's girlfriend and future wife, was found not guilty and released, but Marie, Gallagher's girlfriend and future wife, was sentenced to several years in jail.

Not all that long afterwards I officiated at the McGuinness wedding, which took place across the border in Buncrana, my hometown, because Martin was on the run at that time. A few years later, after Marie was released from prison, I was due to officiate at her wedding to Gallagher, but it clashed with a spiritual retreat I was booked into – I had gone off to think and to ponder if I should leave the priesthood and get married myself.

It was the pre-existing relationship between Duddy, Gallagher and me that would result in us forming the hub of the contact between the British government and the IRA over the next thirty years. This backchannel, as it came to be known, wasn't established in any planned, formal manner. In fact, serendipity played a large part. Frank Lagan was talking to Duddy on a regular basis, Duddy regularly talked to me, I talked to Lagan, and Duddy and I talked to Gallagher. Lagan would have recognised Duddy's political insights as being not far from his own, while both would have seen me engage with matters arising out of the conflict. The three of us would have viewed Noel Gallagher as someone who had an interesting insight into republican history. The fact that we already had these contacts made us natural partners in the backchannel.

It was Lagan who arranged an initial meeting between Frank Steel and/or Michael Oatley and Brendan Duddy. Steel was the most public MI6 person in the North in those years and had worked closely with Lagan in Belfast before Lagan was moved to Derry. MI6 was the leading security agency in the North in the early 1970s. As well as the gatherers of information and the overseers of intelligence systems and operations, MI6 was also the diplomatic outreach on behalf of the government.

Oatley, also of MI6, had been posted to Belfast in early 1973, notionally as assistant political adviser to Willie Whitelaw, and he soon became convinced that there was a need for dialogue with the Provisional IRA. He was charming and had all the qualities that make for a good diplomat (spy) in that you knew who he really was, for whom he worked and what he was trying to extract from any conversation, but you still trusted that he was a sympathetic diplomat who only wanted the best for the situation in which we all found ourselves. My experience of British diplomats was that they either had a quiet disdain for the North and for the Troubles, or that they fell in love with the place, with its people and with the puzzle that is its history. Some of those who fell in love with the place also wanted to become saviours and solvers of the Troubles. Oatley developed some of those salvific traits.

Duddy spent many hours with Oatley and others from the British side. In 1972, a short time before the backchannel came into being, the British government had flown a small group of representatives from the IRA to London for a poorly prepared snap encounter at Cheyne Walk. Jonathan Powell refers to the meeting in his book *Talking to Terrorists* and says that there had been a prior meeting on the Derry/Donegal border, which resulted in a small group of IRA men being flown to London to meet with the Secretary of State Willie Whitelaw. He says that there was no meeting of minds, with the IRA demanding that the British leave Ireland by 1975 and Whitelaw saying that would not happen. Powell also says that when the IRA made the encounter public, it alarmed the unionist community that such a meeting had happened, and, as a result, serious political damage was done to Whitelaw.

If Duddy spent hours talking with Oatley, he equally spent hours talking with Gallagher and me. To understand Duddy, it is necessary to understand how he communicated. He spoke in paragraphs. He found it nigh impossible to say anything directly or simply. He layered everything. That quality was both his strength and his weakness. It was his strength in that he was persistent and dogged and insightful. His energy levels for talking were phenomenal. It was his weakness in that a meeting that should have taken thirty minutes at the most would last an hour and a half. It drove many people to distraction and convinced many others that he was what Derry people called a 'spoofer', someone who talks a lot without much substance.

I didn't agree with that assessment. I was once asked how I

would summarise the backchannel negotiations and I said that I would credit Brendan Duddy with bringing about negotiations between the IRA and the British that occurred in 1975. It took good skills and persistence to initiate and implement a series of talks between two opponents who were so cagey of each other and, for different reasons, terrified of attracting opprobrium from their membership or from the public and media who had not yet come to the opinion that republicans and the British government had to negotiate a way out of the violence and into politics.

Of the three of us who would make up the backchannel, Duddy and I had no formal standing, although Gallagher had a relationship within the broad republican organisation of the IRA/ Sinn Féin. But Frank Lagan had standing and authority and if he thought that a backchannel between the IRA and the government was necessary and that it was better done through people like us, who had no direct connection with a political party, that advice carried some weight. It turned out that we would not be the only backchannel in existence over the years, but the difference was that we were never exposed publicly; the media never knew about us until after our usefulness was at an end. There were other individuals and groups who had similar good intentions, but they did not always have good credentials, in that their suggestions quite often overreached their ability to deliver. These other backchannels regularly broke down because the necessary secrecy didn't last a sufficient time to allow for trust or credibility to establish itself. Trust – about confidentiality and the assurance of no leakage into the public glare – is vital and it grows slowly, agonisingly so. In any such relationship, trust was at a premium, not just between the protagonists themselves, but also between them and the backchannel.

The idea that bonded Duddy, Gallagher and I together was that a stoppage to the killing and the bombing demanded a negotiated agreement between the main combatants – the IRA and the British government as manifested in the British Army and the police. That did not mean that other parties, including the Irish government and the unionists, did not have a role to play. What it did mean was that a successful initiative could only be built after an agreed cessation of violence and the organisations that held the greatest sway over violence were the IRA and the British government. However, that analysis would not have been mainstream when we started out and didn't hold much traction within the political world.

For the first few years of the backchannel, the expression that best describes the situation is that 'we lived in each other's pockets'. The venue for our meetings was mostly Duddy's house. That suited Duddy because he could simultaneously juggle the political exploration and his businesses, which, as well as the chip shop, included three or four clothes shops, a restaurant and part ownership of a hotel. The downside was that Gallagher and I often had to wait while Duddy attended to a banking or a staffing issue. While, for me, that was annoying and stretched my patience, it was destructive to Gallagher's business, which suffered badly from a lack of attention. Duddy, however, was an expert at rationalising the situation and occasionally berated us for not sufficiently dedicating ourselves to the seriousness and the importance of the project.

Duddy had a propensity and a passion for politics. He had been deeply involved in one of the main committees involved in the civil rights movement in Derry in the late 1960s and early 1970s, although I got the impression, listening to himself and others, that he was not given the stature that he thought his political insights and analysis deserved. He believed that he had a good political mind, which he had, but amongst a group of hardened political heavyweights with their own well-developed egos, he found it hard to make the impression and have the influence he would have liked.

The only public recognition that Duddy ever received from the British for his work in the backchannel that I am aware of is a few pages in *Talking to Terrorists*, which argued for governments talking and negotiating with opponents, even those described as terrorists. Powell was Tony Blair's right-hand man in the negotiations that brought about the Good Friday Agreement. The fullest and most informed account of Duddy's thirty years working behind the scenes is outlined in the book *Deniable Contact* by Dr Niall Ó Dohertaigh, professor of history at the University of Galway. Duddy's diary and papers were gifted to the university a few years before he died. Early in the pages of that book there is a question of whether the backchannel was a compound of people or a single person who availed of the support of some others. Ó Dohertaigh decided on the latter, which is unfortunate because it distorts the whole story. While it is true that Duddy was central and vital to the story, it is also true that he would never have been in place as an intermediary in the 1980s and 1990s without Noel Gallagher and me.

Duddy, Gallagher and I made a strange threesome. It was the political situation that brought us together and kept us together. This relationship between three very different men would probably not have lasted for so long had it not been for the Troubles. And when the task it set itself was seen to be done, the relationships didn't hold together.

The strength of the backchannel during the thirty or more years of its existence was the secrecy we were able to maintain. That length of secrecy was unusual, probably unique, in Northern Ireland. Most events and meetings came into the public forum sooner rather than later. We were helped by the fact that the bulk of investigative journalists who had come to the North to report on the civil rights movement and the beginning of the Troubles had stopped coming to Derry. The hotel where they usually rested their heads, the City Hotel, and which doubled as their 'watering hole', was blown up by the IRA in May 1972. Its location in the city centre had made it convenient for covering the happenings in the Bogside and on the west bank of the River Foyle, where most of the trouble was happening.

The secrecy that was maintained during all those years was not easy on our families. They were generally aware of what was happening and yet were not able to talk or share this with their friends. That was particularly the case for the Duddy family, in whose house strange meetings would often take place. They could not talk to anyone about the comings and goings of some people whose faces they would recognise from television and newspapers, and others whom they had never seen before but whose names they would have heard in conversations. They also had to put up with the regular presence of myself and Noel Gallagher, who expected to be supplied with cups of tea and buns. All of that may initially have had an attractive air of excitement and even danger, but over thirty years that early excitement would have waned.

Duddy was dominant and often domineering. Everything had to circulate around his needs and serve the project – bringing peace to Ireland. It must have been very difficult for his wife and children to stand against the drive for Irish freedom and peace. They had little separation, privacy or distance between their lives and the efforts to bring peace. Perhaps it wouldn't have been as demanding if the duration had been shorter.

In 1975 a ceasefire and the negotiations took place between the IRA and the British government, brokered in large part by Duddy. The hope was that, if the two parties could be persuaded to be in the same room together, with time and familiarity they would construct a process that would bring the violence to an end and replace it with an approach that would lead to a political agreement. Duddy had travelled far and talked long to persuade the British that they needed to enter a dialogue with the IRA. He had also been introduced and accredited to Ruairí Ó Brádaigh, the then president of Sinn Féin, by Noel Gallagher. In turn, Ó Brádaigh introduced and accredited Duddy to the IRA Army Council.

Our backchannel effort to initiate these negotiations began not all that long after the disastrous Cheyne Walk meeting, and this new attempt was faced with an understandable caution towards any new proposals that the government and the IRA would begin serious talks. Duddy was the point man with the British, meeting and discussing with those strange, conglomerate beings who are diplomats, civil servants and secret agents rolled into one. That is probably not peculiar to the British system, but it is one in which it has long experience. The home of a Quaker outside Limavady, another house called Laneside on the shores of Belfast Lough and occasionally somewhere in London were the most used venues for these meetings. Oatley, Steel, James Allen and Robert Browning are some of the British names and personalities attached to the beginning of the contacts, ceasefire and negotiations that lasted for the best part of 1975. Mostly it was only Duddy and whoever was the current lead for the British who met, although I did go with Duddy to Laneside on a few occasions.

During the 1975 negotiations, which took part in Duddy's house, Gallagher, Duddy and I were not allowed into the room when the meetings were in session. Our role was to get people to and from the meetings and to ensure that the neighbours and the media were kept in the dark. Dealing with the neighbours was reasonably simple in that there was a substantial wall around Duddy's house, and the few neighbours who would have taken the time to look would have become used to seeing Gallagher and me going in and out of there on a near daily basis. Even the task of keeping media interest away was not as difficult as it might sound. The British and Sinn Féin had established a diversionary second-level set of meetings in Belfast, at Stormont Castle, to distract the press from the Derry venue. A few well-known Sinn Féin figures, mostly Máire Drumm and Proinsias Mac Áirt, occasionally went to meet with a few officials from the Northern Ireland Office (NIO). It was a ploy that kept media eyes looking in the wrong direction. It was also helpful that RUC Chief Superintendant Frank Lagan was instrumental in setting up those negotiations and kept a watchful eye on proceedings, providing transport on a few occasions when it appeared that it might be dangerous for us to drive an IRA man through an army checkpoint to a meeting on a particular day.

Aside from the input I had in discussions between Duddy, Gallagher and myself, my main role in those negotiations was that of a 'go for'. When no one else was available or there was a riskier cross-border journey to be undertaken, I was sent for. I drove Billy McKee, who was on the IRA Army Council in 1975, and Ruairí Ó Brádaigh across the Irish border to negotiation meetings on several occasions.

Duddy liked having me around. He was slightly superstitious. My clerical collar was a good foil, but I also think that there was a modicum of comfort and reassurance for all those men, including the British, to have a priest attached to the effort. The Irish are not the only ones who are superstitious and who like a measure of moral balm.

I must have become more friendly with Browing than with Oatley and the other British officials during that period, because I recently came across a letter from Browning's wife sent to me from Oman. She had come to Derry at some stage and I probably introduced her to the work I and others were doing at the time in the Northlands Addiction Centre. She wrote of their transfer to Oman, of their house there, of their plans to return to England in time to get their children into school. She also wished me well in my work with alcoholics and drug addicts. The most vivid memory I have of Browning himself was a conversation we had after the 1975 talks broke down. He told me that MI6 were leaving or being pulled out of the North and that I should realise that nothing of political significance would happen unless and until people like him came back. He was telling me that he and his kind were the John the Baptists, the precursors, preparing the road for the politicians. What he and I didn't know at the time was that MI6, who were attached to the Foreign Office, were to be replaced by MI5, the Home Office.

As part of the 1975 negotiations between the British and the IRA, I was asked to drive to Dublin on a number of occasions to relay messages and receive instructions to be delivered to the negotiators. I have a strong memory of one such incident. I drove to the capital knowing only that I was to meet up with someone in a car park near Beaumont Hospital. I was surprised at the youthfulness of the person who turned up and who proceeded to drive me deep into a large housing estate. He knocked at the door of a nondescript house and a man I didn't recognise opened the door. We were led into a kitchen where the man removed a toupee and it was only then that I realised it was Dáithí Ó Conaill, the then Chief of Staff and main strategist of the IRA.

Soon afterwards, Seamus Twomey, the Belfast IRA leader, who had a reputation for ruthlessness, arrived at the house. I had to sit in the kitchen while those two discussed the messages I had delivered and whatever response I was to be tasked with carrying back. Strangely, I remember their discussion but not the message that I was relaying from the negotiators who were meeting in Derry.

The three men who represented the IRA during those six months of negotiations were Ruairí Ó Brádaigh, Billy McKee and Joe McCallion. Joe was the only Derry man among them and the only one I previously knew. His family lived in the Long Tower parish and as the violence increased in the area, I had occasion to talk and intercede with him on more than a few occasions. When Frank Lagan rang me early one morning to find out about two soldiers who, reportedly, had wandered into the Bogside late at night and been lifted and held captive by the IRA, it was to McCallion that I went, and it was from McCallion that I got an assurance that the soldiers would not be hurt and would be released. He was always courteous and helpful where possible. I considered him very bright and thoughtful, if elusive. I never knew his history in the IRA. I was never clear how he had achieved the status to be a member of the Army Council, although I think he once told me that he was Dáithí Ó Conaill's blue-eyed boy.

It is only recently that someone pointed out to me that the two soldiers wandering into the Bogside and being captured had happened on the morning of the Cheyne Walk talks. The insinuation was that the two soldiers were both a decoy and hostages against some possibility that the British would arrest a section of the IRA Army Council when they had them in London. Maybe. Paranoia was a constant presence in those days. I wouldn't discount the idea fully because I remember being relaxed about the safety of the two soldiers as I had been allowed to go and see them, and I don't remember them being overly fearful for their lives.

The insinuation that the soldiers were guarantors for the safe passage of the IRA leadership raises two questions. Did Frank Lagan, the chief of police in the area from where the helicopter picked up a strong IRA contingent to go to the London meeting, not actually know about the Cheyne Walk meeting, or was he simply using me and others as a guarantee that the soldiers would remain safe? Joe McCallion spent a considerable time talking to me that day and yet did not give the slightest indication that anything was happening in London. Even in those days I had an inkling that not everything was as it was presented, and as the years passed, I came to know the enormity of the subterfuge that was inherent in our violent conflict.

McCallion never had the profile that Martin McGuinness and others had, something that he would probably have seen as an advantage. Neither did he have the full respect of local members of the IRA. I was never sure if that was because they were annoyed that he was on the Army Council or because they didn't fully trust him. I knew that he and McGuinness had been friends at one time, but by 1975 there was tension between them. McCallion's lower profile allowed the media and indeed the local community to project onto McGuinness a status and a control that he really gained only after the 1975 ceasefire ended. McCallion's authority and his membership came to the same end as all those who were part of the 1975 negotiations. They were replaced by a grouping who were younger, mostly Northern and had probably been wary of and even antagonistic to the ceasefire and the negotiations.

The second of the group, Billy McKee, looked like my father. He had a similar build and square face. In fact, on one occasion we used my father's driving licence to get him across the border so that he could get to a meeting with the British. McKee was a daily Mass-goer, and although he was known in the mid-1970s as the hardest man in the Provos, because I was a priest, he was always very respectful of me. I found him to be the incarnation of that paradox between the ill-formed, non-violent tenets of Catholicism and physical-force Irish republicanism. It is interesting that while he became an icon to the small, fragmented groups of republicans who continue to believe that violence is the only way to force the British government out of Ireland, and accused some of his former colleagues of betraying the cause, he himself sat down to negotiate with the British in these early stages of the conflict.

The third member of the group was Ruairí Ó Brádaigh. I found it difficult to warm to Ó Brádaigh, even though Noel Gallagher always spoke warmly of him. One can be coloured by unimportant matters as much as by great and significant ones.

Ó Brádaigh liked his food. On a couple of occasions that I was sent to pick him up and bring him to meetings in Derry, he was in the middle of eating a meal. Half an hour or more later, he was still eating, with little regard for what hurry or appointments I might have had. I saw him as having a network of houses across Ireland that watered and fed him to a very high standard and that he had been at it for so long that he took it all for granted. I probably attached too much importance to this behaviour but, rightly or wrongly, I marked him down as being spoiled and pampered while giving the impression of being a martyr for the cause.

It was thought that Ó Brádaigh was the main author of *Éire Nua*, the policy document of the Provisional IRA that formulated the organisation's demands to the British. I admired some of its ideas, seeing it as a starting proposition that could be modified and enlarged in any set of negotiations. It was a substantial document that contained some innovative propositions, but the main thrust of it was that the British should announce a date when they would withdraw from Ireland and a federal system of government be put in place. The IRA didn't expect the British to leave immediately, but a definite withdrawal date would be enough to bring about a cessation of violence. The idea was that each Irish province would have a devolved assembly that would participate in a Dáil located in Athlone rather than Dublin. The Ulster assembly would be 'an Ulster Parliament for the Ulster people. The Unionist-orientated people of Ulster would have a working majority within the province and would therefore have considerable control over their own affairs. That power would be the surest guarantee of their civil and religious liberties.' I found it an interesting and informative document.

The British were represented in the 1975 negotiations by Michael Oatley, James Allen and Robert Browning. Oatley had the codename Mountain Climber, but I can't remember Allen or Browning having one. The meetings took place once or twice a week over a period of six months before collapsing.

10

Changing Times

THERE HAS BEEN LOTS WRITTEN about the period of the long ceasefire and the negotiations. Certainly, the accepted view is that the British engagement in the talks was a ruse to militarily weaken the IRA, rather than an actual attempt to make peace. The source of this theory is the memoir of the then Secretary of State for Northern Ireland, Merlyn Rees. He writes that his government had no intention of acceding to any of the requests from the IRA. The British tactic was to elongate the ceasefire and, if possible, divide opinion amongst republicans and reduce their capability to wage a guerrilla campaign. Another view is that the IRA was extreme and unrealistic in its demands and there was no way a British government would accede to their stipulations, such as a withdrawal from Ireland.

Some recent analysis is more nuanced. It has been suggested that Harold Wilson, the then prime minister of the UK, wanted an exit strategy to be developed that would lead to a slow but irreversible withdrawal from the island of Ireland, and that it was the width and depth of opposition from elements within the army, police and political unionism, coupled with a fear that loyalist violence would be very difficult to control, that prevented Wilson from having his way. According to this narrative, what Rees wrote in his memoir was no more than a cover for the more radical discussions that took place.

The counterargument is that after the 1975 negotiations collapsed, the new British Secretary of State, Roy Mason, discarded any policies that defined the Troubles in the context of historical and political ideology, and implemented a strategy called the 'Ulsterisation' of the Troubles. Its purpose was to remove the historical narrative and replace it with a criminal one. That narrative held that the IRA and any opposition to the legitimacy and behaviour of the state arose and was sustained solely from criminal intent.

My judgement is that what happened that year was worthy and substantial but that the process lacked the subtlety and the inclusiveness that such a complex and historical issue needed. It was good to have the two main combatants sit down and discuss the problems and the options over a six-month period, but the engagement needed to be more inclusive and be cognisant, not just in theory, of the opinions and policies of others who had historically been part of the menu that is Anglo-Irish affairs.

I believe that the leadership of the IRA was willing and sincere in exploring the possibilities of an agreement that would address and bring the conflict to an end. The British negotiators who came to that small room in Derry over a period of months in 1975 were doing their best and were strongly committed to finding a way out of conflict. But the small room was hermetically sealed from the world and from the range of outside and important opinions. The Irish government, who were the legitimate voice of the Irish people, had no input and no influence. The non-republican nationalist politicians, the SDLP, who in those years spoke for the greatest numbers, had no input or influence. Unionism, a vital key, also had no input or influence.

That plethora of political parties and governments is, of course, akin to the amalgam of what negotiated the Good Friday Agreement, which means that in principle the same result could have been achieved in 1975. Which raises the question as to why what happened at the end of the 1990s couldn't and didn't happen in the mid-1970s. I have heard the argument made that there hadn't yet been enough death and mayhem and it would take another twenty years to convince both sides that there would be no military victory and a settlement would have to be devised. Unfortunately, there may be some truth to that proposition, but I also think there were other reasons. The main one may have been the political obsession with the theory that the middle ground and moderate politics had to form governance structures that would marginalise and isolate the extremes. That theory was encouraged and sustained by a mindset of moral condemnation against violence that was not validated by an equally vigorous effort to construct and promote alternatives. It wasn't only the Churches who had that responsibility. Business, academia and media were all negligent and self-protective. But with my background, my disappointment was with the Churches, which were justifiably pertinent on the condemnation of violence, but slow, timid and lazy on encouraging and devising discussions and processes that might have led to alternatives.

Martin McGuinness was significant in the above events and discussion by his absence. He was not central to any of it and if a judgement were to be made about his attitude, it would be that he was antagonistic to the ceasefire and the negotiations. He never confirmed it himself, but I heard from a few sources that he was warned by the Army Council that his negativity had been noted; he was told that if he continued to discuss and complain amongst the volunteers about the ceasefire, he could find himself facing a court martial.

My memory is that, in those years, McGuinness was cynical about politics in general and cautious about negotiating with the British government. I think he was still in the full flush of war and believed, in his own words, in the 'cutting edge of the IRA'. Years later I put it to him that during those years he had little appetite for politics and that he had told me on a few occasions that when the war and the fighting was over, he would want to get involved in market gardening, with a bit of fly fishing thrown in. His response was that he had always been interested in politics from his youth; he was surprised at my impression. I would still claim that my memory is correct, and that his interest in politics was something that grew over time.

The ending of the 1975 ceasefire saw the slow demise of the then leadership of the IRA, which was replaced with McGuinness and others. Ó Brádaigh's influence probably suffered most as the 'young Turks', as they became known, developed and implemented their own strategy. The tension between the old and the new would eventually lead to Ó Brádaigh and a small number of his supporters walking out of a Sinn Féin convention that had decided to discontinue a policy of abstentionism from Dáil Éireann. That small group established the Continuity IRA, continuing to promote the policies of 'Éire Nua' while carrying out attacks on the army and the police. Ó Brádaigh died in 2007.

Billy McKee's profile also receded as the 'young Turks' became more prominent. He gave a few interviews to the media, continuing to promote the right of the Irish to militarily resist the presence of the British government in Ireland. His blessing and approval seemed to be keenly sought by the dissident groups who broke away from the leadership of the IRA in the 1990s.

Joe McCallion withdrew completely. He worked a market stall in Derry city and increasingly devoted himself to helping people who suffered from alcohol and drug problems. Many articles about the IRA in those years, and more specifically about the 1975 ceasefire and the negotiations between the two sides, don't name him or refer only to a third person. I don't think he ever gave an interview or made a public statement about this time or the role he played. My instinct is that he had decided that if he and McGuinness were to live in the same city, then he had better fade into obscurity as Martin became more prominent. I knew McCallion for many years but never fully knew his story. He may have been the smartest and most astute of that small group of men who formed the Army Council in those years, and it is unfortunate that his analysis and opinion of the negotiators and the negotiations have never been garnered. It would provide a primary source for a project that might have, and maybe should have, changed the unfortunate events of the coming years.

My own relationship with McGuinness had started with small obligements, one to the other. We were of an age and had come into local public prominence at the same time. I often asked him to stop youngsters being 'put out' – being given the option of leaving Derry or being shot. Being shot usually meant a kneecapping, but occasionally being shot dead. Often the kneecapping would have been, in my eyes, for minor misdemeanours, or more often the young person involved was part of a very disrupted family.

McGuinness would often have had the 'sentence' rescinded, but when he was unsuccessful, he would have had the courtesy to let me know. Sometimes the roles were reversed. When he was worried that a drug pusher was going to be shot dead and asked me to intervene, I got the person into treatment because, as well as pushing drugs, he was addicted himself. The death threat was lifted. The violence was a reality that had to be lived with, with men and boys and a smaller number of girls joining the IRA, men, boys and girls arrested and jailed, and soldiers and police and jeeps and tanks constantly on the streets. While it was understood that there wasn't much any of us could do to change that day-to-day reality, we could work to make it a little less harsh.

I spent some of my time in one of the local police stations or in Ballykelly Army base visiting young boys at the behest of their mothers and fathers. At other times it was intervening with the IRA so a young man would be allowed to stay at home rather than be 'put out'. Sometimes it was trying to quell a riot or prevent it from ever happening.

It was more infrequent, but not unknown, for a more serious, even a murderous attack to be prevented. Chief Superintendent Frank Lagan asking me to intervene to prevent the IRA ambushing police on the Strand Road would have been one such occasion. I can't remember exactly when that happened, but I am certain that the attack was to be from behind a wall at Magee College, which overlooks the Strand Road in Derry. I don't remember if it was to McGuinness himself that I spoke to get the attack called off, but the fact that the other local leaders knew of my close relationship with McGuinness gave me a status and authority that others might not have had. I couldn't claim that it worked the other way around but knowledge that McGuinness was friendly and trusted by one of the parochial priests would not have done his status as the 'trustworthy' and 'decent' one any harm. It wasn't that I was ignorant of the apparent contradiction in my position. If I was opposed to and condemned violence, then how did I justify a friendship with a known 'terrorist'?

My relationship with the IRA was once questioned in a very concrete manner. The British Army included in its ranks religious chaplains, ministers and priests, who supplied pastoral support and guidance to the troops. Some of these were full-time members of the army, but the Catholic ones were more often diocesan or religious priests who signed up for a short period. When they arrived in Derry, they sometimes made themselves known to the local priests and occasionally would come to the parochial house for lunch or dinner. One such chaplain told me that it was my duty to inform the authorities, the army and the police, of the people who were involved and active in the IRA. His argument was that since I was involved with the parish youth club, I would know the young men who joined, and he believed that it was my civic responsibility and, more importantly, my moral duty to assist the authorities to defeat the terrorists. Even though I asked him to leave the house and not return, the suggestion did have a moral core and demanded a satisfactory answer, not for the army chaplain but for me personally.

The moral conundrum was never too deeply buried. It didn't unduly worry me, and I was reasonably content with my own independent views and actions, but I was conscious of the grey areas and the apparent contradictions. During the volatility and the drama, it is easy enough to justify and even fool yourself that your moral compass is working properly. Years later, when I had some downtime with no official or designated role, I tried my hand at writing a script and aspects of such a moral question arose within it. Writing had never come easy to me. In fact, I had a strong block, based on a belief that previous efforts revealed a heaviness and stodginess that made for bad composition. The script never saw the light of day, but the following is an extract from it that gives a flavour of some of the moral dilemmas faced by the IRA and by me because of my relationship with people who espoused and practised violence. The Duggan character is an amalgam of McGuinness and McCallion, and Fr Stephen is a version of me. In this scene, the moral dilemma is viewed from the IRA perspective and was an effort on my part to answer the army chaplain and maybe some of my own perplexities. The scene is a confrontation between the priest and the IRA man over the execution of a boy:

Duggan: I can see I'm in trouble. Look, I didn't want it to happen. I tried to stop it but the evidence was there. He admitted it. He was getting fifty pounds for every piece of information. I have a tape if you want to hear it.

Fr Stephen: And you think that justifies what I saw last night? A young fella lying in the middle of a drain with a bullet in his head. You torture him and put a bullet in his brains and you think that's justified because he got a few lousy pounds from the police.

Duggan (quietly): He wasn't tortured.

Fr Stephen: What do you mean he wasn't tortured? If that wasn't torture then I don't know what the fuck you mean by torture. He's stripped naked, he's tied, he's blindfolded. And you didn't even get him a priest. You call yourself a Catholic and you didn't even get him a priest.

Duggan: And what were you going to do? Hear his confessions and walk out of the room and say 'you can shoot him now, boys'? Wise up, Father.

Fr Stephen: You could have let him go. You could have put him out of the town for a time. For God's sake, he was only a child.

Duggan: He joined the IRA. He knew what he was getting into. You don't inform on other people who end up in jail. If he had come and told us what he had done, he wouldn't have been shot.

Fr Stephen: How do you live with yourself being part of an organisation that shoots its own people at the drop of a hat? I suppose if you thought I was giving information you would shoot me too. You told me it would be all right, that he wouldn't be shot. How do you think I'm going to face his mother after letting her think it would be OK?

Duggan: I didn't tell you that. I told you I would do whatever I could. That's what I told you.

Fr Stephen: You could have stopped it. If you had said 'no' they wouldn't have shot him.

Duggan: Who the hell do you think I am? Would you grow up. There's a war on, Father. And it's going to get worse. There are no nice wars. You think you have it rough because you have to go and face his mother. I happen to know his mother too and she is going to blame me. And she'll probably hate me the rest of her life. I have to live with that. (pause)

I wouldn't say you are not annoyed about the young fella but you're also annoyed about how you look. (putting on an accent) 'Go and see wee Fr Doherty. He'll sort you out. Well there's a lot of things you can't sort out. Look, I happen to believe in what the movement is doing. It's not pleasant at times and it is going to get worse, but at least it's getting us up off our knees and that's more than what the Catholic Church ever did. Oh, it's grand for you. You can come barging in here at any time and give out to me about an informer being shot and you can go and have nice wee chit-chats in the officers' mess. I don't have that privilege; none of the rest of us have that privilege. You don't have to take sides, Father. The rest of us do. Read your history books. The only thing that brings about change is the gun. If we put away the guns now, we are back on our knees. The only reason you're invited to wine and cheese parties with the Brits is because the IRA have guns. If the IRA put the guns away tomorrow, you'd die of hunger. They are using you, Father. They use everybody, they have been doing it for centuries. They are brilliant at it. If the IRA stop, then it all goes back to where it was. Well I'm not going back and those young fellas out on the streets are not going back. And if they intern me or shoot me tomorrow, there's plenty to take my place. (quieter) Look. I wish Paul McLaughlin hadn't been shot. I wish there was a different way. You can believe me or not,

but I did try. He was a stupid young fella, and
the bottom line is if the IRA let people tout, they
won't last a week.

They lasted more than a week. The words I put into Duggan's
mouth are not without merit and substance, but they were not
subtle enough or layered enough to answer the moral question
that arose from the army chaplain's assertion that I had a duty
to tell the authorities the names of those involved in the IRA.
Or that I was too close to the IRA or at least to people who had
made the decision to join the IRA and who should now be seen
and treated as terrorists.

There had already been six deaths in two years arising from the
Troubles within the small parish where I worked. Six deaths –
Billy McGreanery, Eugene McGillan, Colm Keenan, Paul Giffin,
Seamus Brown and Kathleen Feeney – which all took place within
half a mile of each other and within the first two years of the
1970s. At the corner of the street where I was living, an army
sanger, or armoured guard post, had been established. There was
always a rifle protruding from this look-out point. I passed it ten,
twenty, maybe forty times a day. As I mentioned previously, I had
a phobia about being shot in the head, so the few steps from my
car to the front door of the parochial house that I went into every
night was the worst part of my day. This small area, this small
parish to which I was attached was a snapshot, a reflection of the
spiralling violence and the political vacuum that was the Troubles
in the 1970s. It was also a maelstrom of moral confusion for
many people, me included.

Condemnation of violence by the Churches was repetitive

and ineffective and resulted in the accusation mainly from the republican side that there was a hierarchy of condemnation. The pacifism argument was noticeable by its absence, save from a very small number of Quakers who had moved over from England to live in places like Derry. They were admired by the locals for their social work and their efforts to mediate peace. The theology advocated by Tom O'Gara, mentioned earlier for a different kind of ministry, was academically interesting and attractive but probably much too far ahead of its time to have any practical relevance. The community activism to which I had a strong attachment was helpful in small pockets but almost irrelevant within the context of a warlike conflict raging on the streets.

The politics of the Troubles was mostly built on the premise of finding a settlement between the centre-ground parties. The British and Irish governments met and discussed and mostly disagreed on the cause and the solution. The only coherent policy was greater security and the growth of the middle ground, which, supposedly, would marginalise and nullify the IRA and the loyalist paramilitaries. If I ever agreed with that premise, I certainly did not agree with it as the years passed and after what I had seen and experienced. I did not agree that the IRA could be marginalised by the growth of the centre ground. Neither did I think that it would be weakened by condemnations coming from the Churches. I also didn't think that the British government had any clear vision: they certainly had the military power to wipe out the IRA, but to have done that would have meant enormous death and horrendous social destruction and, perhaps more pertinently, reputational damage.

I had been home on holiday from Rome in the late 1960s when Jack Lynch made his famous statement that the Irish government would not stand idly by while the people of Derry and the North were under threat. I had now been living among those people for a few years and could not detect any clarity or impulse from that government to bring the conflict to an end. The old and unfinished Anglo-Irish conflict was once again at the centre of the Troubles and the only way I could see the fighting and the killing coming to an end was for the two primary killing machines, the IRA and the British government, to agree to let politics perform its primary function, which is to prevent conflict and differences in society from degeneration into violence and to bring resolution to entrenched political divisions. The logic of that was that the two main protagonists had to be at the centre of the discussions that would hopefully lead to a resolution.

I still can't be certain whether I was holding a moral position or a political pragmatic one, while telling myself that one didn't necessarily contradict the other. I can't be sure that I ever fully countered the army chaplain's accusation, but I comforted myself with the assertion that he should have been applying the same standards to himself and his position within the British Army. The most likely answer, and probably the most truthful one, is that I was carried along by the sweep of events. Included in that sweep was the rise of McGuinness in stature and authority within the republican movement and the fact that, at that time, he and I had a close relationship.

The failure of the IRA and British negotiations in 1975 brought about change. It included the demise of the older IRA leadership, the resignation of Frank Lagan as a protest over placing the RUC in the primary position in the battle with the IRA and loyalist paramilitaries, and the 'criminalising' of the Troubles introduced by the new Secretary of State, Roy Mason. All of that and more was happening at the macro level.

While all this was going on, on a personal level I was falling in love with Mary Wilson and, along with her and others, establishing a drug and alcohol treatment facility. Mary was the lynchpin in doing the research and structuring the treatment methodologies. My contribution was to go off to Minneapolis for a month to look at some of the developing treatments there.

I have a memory of a discussion I had when I was a seminarian in Rome in which I argued that it was more than likely that at some time in my priestly ministry I would fall in love. I argued that this would enhance my understanding of human love and while it might be painful to reject the consummation of that love, it would deepen my understanding of ministry and my priesthood. What a plonker!

Falling in love was a tsunami within my being. It was a gentle but increasing enjoyment in talking to and being in Mary's company. I found her insights and views of the world and human behaviour intriguing and so, so attractive. The urge to listen to her and have her intelligently introduce me to human insights grew and grew. A few years later we began working together as therapists for addicted people and in all the years I have been around the addiction field I have never met a better therapist. Her personality and her skills kept me grounded and focused. Mary would never have allowed me to get a 'big head' or an undue regard for myself. She has an unshakeable regard for the equality of all people; no one should be idolised. She loved me to bits, but to her, thankfully, I was no idol. Fifty years later I still love listening to her voice and her insights. I suppose I knew I had fallen in love with her when I realised that when I would see her at a Mass I was saying, my heart would jump. I loved saying Mass, the eucharistic celebration, and now I loved Mary, but the norms of the Catholic Church would not facilitate both. Mary and I had a choice to make.

The decision was made that I would leave the priesthood and we would get married. That statement is easily made, but in those days and in that society such a move was a big deal. There were few, if any, priests who had left the priesthood and remained in Derry. Leaving the Catholic priesthood at that time nearly always meant going off to get married and most of the priests who did that went abroad to live and find work. However, I had no intention of leaving the city or my work in the alcohol and drug treatment centre that we had set up. I loved Mary and I loved the work too much for that to happen.

The two other people most affected by this decision were the two I was working with in the backchannel, for very different reasons. Noel Gallagher was due to get married, and I had been asked to be the officiating priest at his and Marie's wedding. I only let him know a few days before the wedding that I was going on retreat and that I had asked my closest priest friend to stand in for me. Gallagher was naturally annoyed, but he accepted that it was my decision.

Brendan Duddy's opposition was much more marked. I had thought that he would shrug it off and was surprised when he asked Joe McCallion, who was still on the Army Council at the time, to talk me out of leaving. I began to realise that he saw my priesthood as an important component of the backchannel, specifically in the relationship with the IRA, providing a comfort blanket to those who believed that the involvement of a priest was a symbol of good intent and integrity. But, more significantly, it was a protection to himself, knowing that there were those, especially McGuinness, who did not fully trust him, and that if a difficult and dangerous moment were to arrive, my priesthood would act as a shield. And such a moment would arrive.

After we got married in 1981, Mary and I continued to work in Northlands, the name we gave to the drug and alcoholic treatment facility we had set up. We also continued to live in Derry and face into some of the awkward consequences of my decision. Awkward in that family, friends and the public generally split into those who found our marrying to be a mistake, or wrong, and those who saw the depth of the love we shared and were sympathetic and supportive. Priests were split between those who tried to talk me out of going through with the marriage because it would be a scandal to the laity and those who were fully respectful and supportive to both Mary and me. There were a few condemnatory letters and phone calls, but the Derry Catholic community, as it was sometimes referred to, if they took it under their notice at all, appeared to welcome the fact that we were staying and working here, unlike many priests who had got married but felt that they had to leave the area or even the country.

The greatest difficulty many people seemed to have was over what to call me. The greeting 'Fr Bradley' often came of their mouth naturally before they realised what they were saying. They and I soon got used to those slips and even to this present day I sometimes get called 'Fr Bradley', quickly followed by an 'Oh dear, sorry.'

Those years quickly slipped into the very tense years of the hunger strikes. The backchannel was still in existence and Brendan Duddy was still meeting with representatives from the British government. Martin McGuinness was no longer an observer to the work of the backchannel but was now the recipient and instigator of any activity between the IRA and the government.

The years of the hunger strikes in 1980 and 1981 were the ones that I found the most disturbing and depressing. The atmosphere, the tension and the hopelessness were suffocating. And what made it even worse is that the deterioration into violence and aggression was predicted and predictable. The government was well warned by those in the backchannel and by many reputable groups within politics and civic society to leave the prisons alone. There had been deals in the past, the most famous with Billy McKee, that led to normal clothing for Troubles prisoners and some recognition of political status, which had brought enough stability to indicate that there was no need to solve a problem that was already stabilised. Even a minimal understanding of Irish history would point to the depth of emotion that the withdrawal of political status would arouse. But the policy of criminalising the Troubles introduced by Roy Mason was further embedded after the breakdown of the 1975 negotiations and augmented by Margaret Thatcher's simplistic analysis.

While I wasn't in the middle of it at that point, I was conscious that the backchannel was at its busiest during the days, weeks and months that the ten hunger strikers died. Occasionally, I dropped into Duddy's or Gallagher's homes, or they came to me, to chat and give an update. It was easy to see the pressure that both were feeling. On one such day I spent an hour or more on Duddy's front porch as he talked on the phone to his contact on the British side. The conversation was conducted, as was the norm when on the phone, in coded language. For the greatest part of that hour, I was trying to remember the code words that Duddy used for the IRA, the British, Margaret Thatcher and himself. Despite my rustiness, it was clear to me that Duddy was not just delivering or receiving messages but was trying to suggest and encourage strategies that would save face for both sides, as well as saving the lives of those still on strike. (A few of the prisoners had already died by that stage.)

I was also aware that Gallagher was regularly travelling up and down the Derry to Belfast road, bringing messages and receiving instructions. The IRA had appointed a few people in Sinn Féin to negotiate on their behalf and they were introduced for the first time to the existence of the backchannel and the personnel involved.

The hunger strikes were hugely important in the history of the Troubles, but I am hesitant to write about them precisely because I was not involved in the communications or the discussions or the negotiations that took place during those harrowing weeks and months. But I had strong opinions about it, even as it was happening. For me, the removal of special status was another blunder by the government in the same category as internment. On the republican side, the death of the strikers enhanced the morale of the IRA but did not lead to any facing by either side into the fundamental issues that constituted the Troubles.

In September 1981 Jim Prior was appointed secretary of state for Northern Ireland. Within a number of months, a settlement was reached, basically granting the prisoners what they had demanded but at the terrible price of ten men dead in prison, a considerable number of army and police killed, and a growing feeling that we were on the brink of civil war.

I met Prior only once, when I was a member of the BBC Northern Ireland Council, which had a consultative role in the governance and output of the BBC. Lucy Faulkner, the wife of the last prime minister of Northern Ireland, was its chairperson. She organised a dinner for Prior and a few members of the council, and I was seated beside Prior. During an intense discussion, he said that although it looked as if the country was on the precipice of civil war, every time he thought it was going to fall over that cliff, the IRA seemed to pull back. And he asked me why the IRA had not put a bomb somewhere like the underground in London, which would have resulted in the Troubles taking on an importance and priority within government that it had not demanded in those days.

There was a stunned silence around the table. I answered that it was Catholic morality that prohibited such an action – it allowed for war and violence but not for indiscriminate killing. But I added that all morality, including Catholic morality, tended to be swept aside by the impetus of violence.

Although I had begun to drift away from the backchannel in the 1980s and didn't, any longer, see myself as part of it, I wasn't able to fully escape. There were people and events that appealed for some intervention or mediation, where some little effort might help to smooth out or eradicate the problem. That was the case when Don Tidey, chairman and chief executive of the Associated British Food Companies in Northern Ireland and the Republic, was kidnapped by the IRA. Stewarts Supermarkets was a subsidiary of Associated British Foods trading in Northern Ireland at the time. One of their executives approached a priest in the Derry diocese, who in turn approached Fr George McLaughlin to explore what could be done to get Tidey released. McLaughlin got in touch with me, and I reluctantly contacted McGuinness. I say reluctantly because I hate kidnappings; there is something extraordinarily repulsive about imprisoning a person and bargaining for money for his/her life or release.

For the following three weeks I became the intermediary between Stewarts and the IRA. It was several days after the kidnapping in Dublin that I was called in, and some more days passed before it was confirmed that the Provisional IRA was the group that had done the kidnapping. I met with the Stewarts representative every three or four days in Fr McLaughlin's house, checking for any updates. He was not the most gracious man I had ever met, but I had to consider that he might have been a reluctant intermediary or messenger and that he was possibly terrified. McGuinness was also not delighted about being pulled into the frame. That may have been because he was feeling exposed, not knowing who was initiating the contact. It might well have been the security services setting him up to take the blame. Or it may be because he had to listen to my sermonising on the evils of kidnapping.

We had advanced to the stage where a meeting had been arranged in a New York café between a representative of the company and an IRA rep. A codeword and a serrated piece of paper were to be the identifiers. However, before that meeting could take place, the Irish security authorities discovered where the kidnapped man was being held and a gun battle ensued in which a young garda and a soldier were tragically shot and killed. Don Tidey was rescued and returned to his family. It was only recently that I read the following report from the *Times* newspaper of 29 June 2008:

Ireland seizes €6m IRA funds from Tidey kidnap

Cash paid by food company to protect its executives from further abduction turns up in dormant terrorist account.

Cash seized from a dormant bank account earlier this year was protection money paid to the IRA on behalf of a British food company following the kidnapping of Don Tidey, one of its executives.

Almost €6m in IRA funds, which had been frozen in a bank account for more than 20 years, was paid into the public coffers in March. A sum of IR£1.7m was initially sequestered by a judge in February 1985 after gardaí were tipped off that it had been paid to the IRA on the orders of Associated British Foods (ABF) to ensure that none of its executives was kidnapped again.

I have no idea if that story is true. I had always been under the impression that any liaison had ended when Don Tidey was rescued. Memory is deceptive, but I don't think there would have been enough time between the serrated paper being handed over and the release of Tidey for that New York meeting to have taken place. If the *Times* story is accurate, then there was probably a second mediation going on simultaneously. That is not outside the realms of possibility. Big business and the IRA were both more than capable of spreading their bets. McGuinness certainly said nothing, and no one ever came back from Stewarts to update me or to say thanks, if not to me, then to Fr McLaughlin. Not even a tin of biscuits!

11

A Crucial Meeting

HIS MOTHER PEGGY'S HOUSE WAS not somewhere I had met Martin McGuinness all that often. Way back in the early 1970s, he had asked me to meet with himself and Dáithí Ó Conaill, then chief of staff of the IRA, and that meeting had taken place in Peggy's house. But those were the very early days of the Troubles, and I was a very young priest who had only been in the Long Tower parish a short time.

At that meeting, Ó Conaill had told me that he wanted to set up a local police force for the Bogside and Creggan, and he was suggesting that I would be a good person to front it. He was concerned that too many people were asking McGuinness and the other leaders of the local IRA to sort out problems that had nothing to do with politics or, as he referred to it, the 'armed struggle'. Things like marriage difficulties, drinking and drug problems, petty crime, family and neighbour's disputes – the everyday realities that had become more intrusive and were growing in volume and seriousness because of the lack of an effective police force. The local RUC station had been closed for years and the police now only came into the area in jeeps, normally accompanied by the British Army. The growing social problems were interfering with the primary task of the IRA, which was to bring the armed struggle to the British government and security forces.

Nothing came of Ó Conaill's suggestion, of course. I was a political cub, but I had enough sense to know what was practical and what was unworkable. I am sure I wouldn't have had the foresight or the confidence to have said it on the night, but neither was I foolish enough to be lifting the burden from the IRA so that they could get on with their shooting and bombing. However, the meeting alerted me to the danger that any involvement in trying to make things better, or at least less bad, for the local community was easily interpreted as support for one or other of the protagonists in the Troubles.

Before McGuinness and I had ever met, Peggy would have told him all about me when I came to the parish. Her people and my people were neighbours and friends. Both families came from the Illies, where I was born and reared. Their family name was Walls, but for the life of me I can't remember if that was their surname or a nickname used to distinguish them from some other family of a similar name, a custom that was common in that part of Donegal. They were probably Doherty, because nearly every family was either Doherty or McLaughlin.

I have a memory of visiting the Walls' house with my father and mother when I was quite a young child. I particularly remember Kitty, Peggy's mother and Martin's granny, a large, handsome woman with a warm, attractive smile. I was shy, very shy, in those days, and on such occasions, going into a strange house with strange people, I normally hid behind my parents' legs, but

I remember being comfortable with Kitty. She had a warmth and charm that made me feel comfortable. Her grandson inherited a strong dose of that charm.

Peggy's younger sister, Mary, was married to my first cousin and was a close friend of two of my sisters. Mary was a beautiful woman, both in looks and in personality, who sadly died of cancer at far too early an age, leaving a large and young family. By that time, Peggy herself had married and moved to Derry.

It was nine o'clock or thereabouts on 23 March 1993 when I knocked on Peggy's door. Noel Gallagher had been at the house just over half an hour earlier. Now, here I was arriving out of the blue.

The original plan had been that two people from the NIO would meet with two people from the republican side. Gallagher was to pick up McGuinness and Gerry Kelly and drive them to Brendan Duddy's house, where they would meet with the British representatives. However, when Gallagher told them that only one person from the British side had turned up, they refused to go. The IRA and Sinn Féin were sticklers for procedure.

What they didn't know was how difficult and frustrating a day it had been for the three of us in the backchannel. The meeting between the British and the IRA had been agreed a few days previously and Duddy had been assured that it would take place and that two representatives of the NIO would attend. But on the morning of 23 March a fax had arrived in Duddy's house, cancelling the meeting.

We knew only too well that Prime Minister John Major was nervous. His government had a slim majority and some of his backbenchers would have been enormously antagonistic to any contact with the IRA. All we could assume was that someone who knew about the proposed meeting, perhaps Major himself, had got cold feet, fearing that the government would not survive media leaks of a meeting between its representatives and the IRA.

After the fax arrived there was a long, frustrated discussion between the three of us who comprised the backchannel. We had kept that channel in existence for over twenty years, despite the caution and self-protection of the British and the suspicions, maybe even the antagonism, of some members of the IRA. The discussion developed into a debate about what we were doing and why we were doing it. It wasn't the first time that we had discussed the rationale for and effectiveness of the backchannel. Were we being used and abused by both sides, by the British and by the IRA? One or other of us had said on more than one occasion that there was a danger that we were being prostituted, used by one or both sides but never fully committed to. That accusation could be levelled at both sides but probably more often at the British. On this occasion I think I might have been the most outspoken, and I might also have been the angriest.

It was almost three years since Peter Brooks had delivered the speech stating that the British had 'no selfish or strategic interest in Northern Ireland' and would not stand in the way of a united Ireland if it was by consent. The written version of that speech was delivered to the IRA through the backchannel, days before it was publicly delivered. Three years later, a long time in politics, an agreement had been reached for both sides to meet for exploratory talks. For the British to pull out at the last minute could have been the death knell for all the work it had taken to get to this tentative arrangement. Apart from anything else, I felt that I wouldn't have the energy to keep going or trying to pick up all the broken pieces that would be the result of such a disappointment.

The three of us in the backchannel had come together based on a belief that the only way the violence could be stopped, and a political accommodation reached, was for the two principal killing machines, the IRA and the British government, to negotiate a way out of violence and into politics. The failure of the negotiations between the IRA and the British in 1975 had left a sour taste in many people's mouths, including my own. Eighteen years later, it could have been a Groundhog Day, with the only difference being that those who were to speak for the IRA and the British government had changed. Duddy, Gallagher and I were the constants.

I had only formally returned to the backchannel shortly before this difficult discussion, having largely absented myself for some years. Although I continued to see Duddy and Gallagher from time to time, and they kept me briefed on anything important that was happening, I had stopped going to the interminable meetings that Duddy insisted on having to either prepare for his meetings with the British or to report back on a meeting that had taken place. He was the face-to-face interlocutor with the British, and if there was ever a man who could, and indeed did, talk for Ireland, it was Duddy. I remained aware of the contacts, the efforts that he and Gallagher were involved in to find a settlement to the hunger strikes, and that McGuinness was now not only the chief negotiator on behalf of the IRA but increasingly seen as one of the most influential members of the republican community.

The reasons for my absence had been complicated. I was suspicious that the British were so self-protective that they spoke with a forked tongue, as much to themselves as to us. They wanted to stay close to this small group in the backchannel because we had a grasp of republican thinking and were leak-proof, in that we had arranged a previous round of negotiations between the two sides without the media ever getting to know who was involved, and had been the intermediaries between the IRA and the government at the time of the hunger strikes and still maintained the confidentiality of it all. At the same time, they were reluctant to make a movement into face-to-face talks with that amalgam of Irish republicanism, which sometimes presented itself as Sinn Féin and at other times as the IRA. I was certain that the British government wanted to keep the backchannel open but in a manner that was politically deniable. The fear of a backlash from influential people within the security services and within their own party, Conservative or Labour, made them fearful.

Another reason for distancing myself was more mundane but much more personal and important – my decision to leave the priesthood and get married. Marriage, children and work all took up a lot of time and this allowed me to drift away from the interminable meetings while still being in touch with the overall picture.

My judgement had been, for a long number of years, that McGuinness would be a key influencer in bringing the IRA to the negotiation table. In the early 1980s, after standing down from working at Northlands Treatment Centre, Mary and I established a small television company called Northland Films. In that role I had attended a few Sinn Féin Party conferences, and observed the interaction between McGuinness, Gerry Adams and the rest of the leadership of the republican movement. I once said to McGuinness that Adams, after delivering conference speeches, always turned to him for approval. His response was that I would be foolish to underestimate Adams.

I also relied on the knowledge and judgement of Noel Gallagher, who had grown up with McGuinness, to understand who was powerful and influential within the ranks of republicanism. He would have said that there were 'harder' men on the Army Council of the IRA, but that none of them had the breadth of backing and influence that McGuinness had.

My hopes for an end to the violence were considerably raised after a conversation I had with McGuinness in the early 1990s, in which he had expressed an opinion that the republican movement had to become peacemakers and move away from violence. However, his attitude to the backchannel had always been sceptical rather than positive. He believed that the 1975 ceasefire and the six-month negotiations with the British had come close to destroying the IRA. That negativity was compounded by his mistrust, even dislike, of Brendan Duddy.

McGuinness and I had a relationship forged in the day-to-day events of the Troubles. It was forthright and sometimes argumentative, but there was an underlying trust that was enhanced by the fact that I was the priest who had officiated at his wedding. Duddy, on the other hand had a personality that grated with McGuinness, who did not like his loquaciousness and regarded his motives as self-interested and egotistical, sometimes describing him as self-serving.

At that meeting in the early 1990s, when McGuinness talked about the need for republicans to become peacemakers, he referred to this dislike of Duddy. He knew that I had not officially been a part of the backchannel for years, but valued my judgement, which was that the opportunity was too great to be ignored or blocked by a clash of personalities. I defended Duddy and his work as best I could but proposed that I would return to the backchannel if that made it easier for him to develop the momentum for peace. And so once again I became part of the threesome.

When the fax came through that the British were pulling out of the March 1993 meeting, I argued that there was no way that the link could continue if the meeting was cancelled. McGuinness had cleared it with the Army Council, and another member of that council (at that stage we didn't know it would be Gerry Kelly) would already be on his way to Derry. The distrust and the fear on both sides was always high. A meeting cancelled at the last moment at this time of mounting expectation would only add to the difficulty of getting the sides together. The last time the British government and the IRA had met face to face was sixteen or more years ago; it had taken years to get this new meeting set up.

To call it off at the last minute would be disastrous for what Duddy, Gallagher and I had been trying to bring about for years. If the British didn't come, I wanted them told that I would no longer be part of the link. I argued that the other two should make it clear that they were of the same mind. Gallagher agreed, as did Duddy, who had put years into meeting, cajoling, arguing with and educating British diplomats, and who would have found it the most difficult to walk away and stay away. The decision was made to send an ultimatum to the British that we would terminate the link if the meeting was cancelled.

After several faxes, Fred faxed back to say that he would meet with Duddy but not with the IRA. That was a further irritant.

I don't know how many faxes went back and forth after that, but by early afternoon Fred contacted us to say that the meeting was back on schedule. To this day I do not fully know why Fred arrived on his own. Our assumption had been that he would be accompanied by either John Deverell, Director of Intelligence in Northern Ireland, who was one of those who died in the chinook helicopter crash on the Mull of Kintyre in June 1994, or Quentin Thomas, a senior civil servant in the NIO. But in the end, no one else came.

Both sides were playing hard to get. The meeting was on, then off, and now it depended on persuading the two republicans that it should happen. It was Duddy who very quickly suggested that I should take Fred to Peggy McGuinness' house. I wasn't dying about the suggestion, but he was right – I was the most likely to be able to persuade McGuinness to take the meeting. I was amazed that Fred agreed to go with me. I was going to drive him into the heart of the Bogside to meet with two of the most senior members of the IRA. Two men who were annoyed that they had been stood up. Fred could have been abducted and used for ransom. I believed that would not happen, but had I been Fred, it would have been at the front of my mind. Yet he didn't object.

I drove Fred to the house and left him in the car while I persuaded McGuinness to hear him out. When McGuinness reluctantly indicated that he would, I fetched Fred and then left him in the kitchen of Peggy's house to make his case to McGuinness and Kelly. It was nerve-wracking sitting in the living room with Peggy, waiting for the outcome of that discussion.

I felt a massive wave of relief when McGuinness emerged from the kitchen with the news that the meeting would go ahead, and I was to tell Gallagher to pick Kelly and himself up in about fifteen minutes. Fred and I drove back to Duddy's house. He was not very forthcoming about how he had changed their minds beyond repeating some of the things I had already said and explaining that while there was great apprehension in government about meeting with the IRA, there was also a strong conviction that both sides had to meet and come to an understanding.

Thirty minutes after leaving the McGuinness house I tapped the ash out of my pipe and walked into the office attached to Duddy's house. There was a large boardroom table. Fred was sitting on the left with Duddy. Gallagher was at the far end of the table. McGuinness and Kelly had arrived and were now sitting beside each other on the right. I was at the top. Someone decided that I was to chair the meeting. Chairing only meant asking Fred to begin and, after a few hours, thanking him and McGuinness and Kelly for coming.

This was the second time in eighteen years that the British and the Provos had met in this house. It was not the same room because the large office-type space hadn't been built when the earlier meetings took place. But then, unlike this night, those meetings had not been a preliminary coming together to explore the possibility of negotiations. Then, it was actual negotiations between the British government and the IRA, which lasted for six months, and McGuinness had not been involved. He was not on the Army Council of the IRA in those early days, nor was he the commanding officer of the IRA in Derry.

Of course, McGuinness had attended the one-off meeting with then Northern Ireland Secretary of State, Willie Whitelaw, in July 1972, which took place in Cheyne Walk in London, but that had only lasted three hours. He had been growing in stature within the local organisation and had been picked out of obscurity to accompany a few of the better-known IRA men to London. Because he had been chosen to go to Cheyne Walk and because he was well respected among the volunteers, he was often put forward as a spokesperson and that profile created the impression that he was the leader of the IRA in Derry. The reality was somewhat different. McGuinness was not kept informed as to how the 1975 talks were progressing. As the months passed, his hostility was expressed more aggressively and more openly. His view was that the British were stringing the talks out to weaken the determination and the capability of the IRA.

Years later I was asked to give a lecture at the University of Liverpool, in which I tried to give some insight into the 1975 negotiations and their consequences. I suggested that advice centres set up in IRA heartlands probably contributed more than anything else to the politicisation of young nationalists and republicans, encouraging the growth of the modern Sinn Féin party. I also noted that although reasonably young and politically inexperienced, my instincts at the time had told me that neither side was well prepared for such an engagement. The IRA was willing and serious, but its bottom line of 'Brits out' was overly fundamental and inadequate in the light of the complexity of the historical problem. But it was a more honest position than the one adopted by the British if, indeed, their primary interest was to weaken the military capability of the IRA; if not, and Wilson actually did have an exit strategy in mind, the depth of opposition to this might simply have been too great for this strategy to have any success.

Following the breakdown of those talks in 1975, in terms of violence and death, what followed was equally bad, if not worse, than what had happened before the ceasefire. There were two very definite political outcomes as well. The first was that the involvement of MI6 in the talks led to tensions within the British administration. Enoch Powell was probably the most articulate and certainly the most persistent in expressing suspicion of the British Foreign Office and its MI6 network. He and others were suspicious that the Foreign Office was much too understanding of Irish history and the Irish narrative, and not properly responsive to the history of unionism and the unionist narrative. In his and many others' views, Northern Ireland was an internal matter and, as such, was the responsibility of the Home Office and MI5. The second outcome was that the IRA went through an internal reorganisation, sidelining those who approved the six-month ceasefire. The then leadership of the IRA – Billy McKee, Seamus Twomey, Ruairí Ó Brádaigh, Dáithí Ó Conaill, Joe McCallion, etc. – collapsed and was replaced by McGuinness, Adams and a more northern-centred influence and membership.

The meeting with Fred in 1993 was not the first time McGuinness had met with a man who held a senior position in the British bureaucracy. In the early 1990s, around the time that I formally returned to the backchannel, Brendan Duddy had arranged a meeting between McGuinness and Michael Oatley to explore the lie of the land, the willingness on either side to meet, talk and negotiate. I was aware that the meeting was taking place but was not fully convinced of its importance.

Duddy and Oatley had grown friendly during the 1975 talks and had stayed in touch in the intervening years. After the breakdown of the negotiations that had taken place in 1975, Oatley had been promoted and became head of MI6 in the Middle East, but Duddy had informed me of his continuing interest in the affairs of Northern Ireland. Perhaps he saw the 1975 negotiations as a missed opportunity to bring an end to violence and conflict, but I was slightly afraid that he had become salvific about the Anglo-Irish conflict and didn't want to give up on contributing to a solution. Whatever his reasons, his ability was never in doubt, and I am sure his knowledge and his conviction would have impressed McGuinness.

On this night of the nearly cancelled 1993 meeting, we were on our second attempt to bring the two warring factions together, and after the near collapse, before a start had even been made, we were in Duddy's large room, gathered around a table, with no script and no agenda but with some hope and a lot of experience. Official government records released after thirty years or so claim that the reason the meeting took place at all was because the government had received a letter from McGuinness saying that the war was over, but that they (Sinn Féin and the IRA) needed help to bring it to an end – the government couldn't ignore such a letter. In other writings, I claimed to have written that letter, so I feel that I should take this opportunity to clarify what happened.

I came back into the backchannel in 1990 and three years later the necessary movement into dialogue and negotiation between the IRA and the British had not materialised. During those three years, a solid negotiating foundation had been constructed, and yet neither of the two protagonists was willing to take the first step onto that foundation. Meetings between John Hume and Gerry Adams had been taking place in Clonard monastery in Belfast for some time. The Hume–Adams document, which was not really a document but an overarching sketch of principles, was floating between Sinn Féin, the SDLP and the Irish government, being modified but not substantially changed. It was like a fire being set in a fireplace, the paper and coal added, but then removed, then set again, without anyone putting a match to it. The three of us in the backchannel had access to most of the comings and the goings, the heightened expectations and the pulling back from those expectations. It was exasperating.

One nondescript morning Duddy and Gallagher arrived at my office and, after another long discussion about the continuing frustration, we decided to pen a letter. When I say I wrote the letter, I mean I wrote the words on the page and had them typed up. The letter was an overview of the desire on both sides to move and the inability to make the move. The statement that the war was over was a psychological, not militaristic assertion. As it came from the backchannel, it meant that there were no signatures on the letter, but any direct messages coming from us could have been interpreted as coming from McGuinness and the IRA. It would be tempting to claim that the letter was an especially clever subterfuge to get a match put to the fire, when in reality it simply reflected our desperation to get the fire lit.

Duddy took the letter to London, where he was meeting Fred a few days later. My memory is that Gallagher, unusually enough, also attended that meeting. I don't know if Duddy and/ or Gallagher added to or reconstructed the letter or, more likely, if Fred presented it as a plea coming from McGuinness. I don't know; I might never know. My regret is that I didn't keep a copy, but then again, with a few exceptions, I kept a copy of very little.

As the meeting started that night in Duddy's large boardroom, I thanked everyone for coming and asked Fred to begin by outlining what the British government was proposing. He talked for the best part of an hour. It was a tour de force. A journey through Anglo-Irish history, connecting it to forty years of unresolved conflict and the need to bring that conflict to an end, not just temporarily but permanently. When he got to the point of what the British would be offering in the negotiations that would have to take place, he didn't promise too much. Britain would not be pushed out of Ireland by force, he said. It had a moral obligation to the unionist population, and it would not turn its back on that position. Neither would it become a persuader for Irish unity. That was the task of the Irish people themselves. But the government was also reading the signs of the times and it was clear that those signs pointed to the unification of the island, over time. Therefore, the British government would not do anything in the coming years to enhance or strengthen the union between Northern Ireland and the UK.

Having sketched the bigger picture, he moved on to the logistics of beginning negotiations. It would be a requirement that the IRA would call a two-week ceasefire, but negotiations could begin after a week. Their best judgement was that secrecy could be maintained for no more than a week. Scotland would be the most likely venue, but Norway was a possibility. John Chilcot, head of the NIO, would not participate initially but would join the discussions after a few days.

Neither McGuinness nor Kelly interrupted this exposition, but as soon as Fred had finished, they put several specific queries to him about his authority and whether it came from the prime minister. Having been assured that he was speaking on behalf of

John Major, they then asked him who else in the government was cognisant of possible negotiations. The questioning continued for nearly an hour, precise, penetrative but polite. Observing only, my judgement was that Fred more than passed the examination. I thought the interrogators were impressed that questions were answered clearly. Difficulties and blockages were acknowledged and nothing extravagant or unrealistic was promised. McGuinness stated that there would be a response in the not-too-distant future. The meeting ended sometime after midnight. McGuinness and Kelly were the first to leave, and just as Fred was about to pull his car out of the driveway to head back to Belfast, I stuck my head in the window and thanked him for his bravery.

It had been a torturous road to get to that night and it was equally torturous from that night to the point at which Sinn Féin became fully embroiled in the political talks with the British and Irish governments and the other northern politicians. But that night weakened the dam that had been stopping the two main combatants from negotiating with each other on how to bring an end to the violence and allow politics to do its job; weakened it enough to reveal to both sides that the charade of not speaking or negotiating with each other could not hold for much longer, especially if the IRA was to respond positively and offer a ceasefire.

Sinn Féin has published its own record of communications between themselves and the British government between October 1990 and November 1993. In that publication the meeting with Fred is reported on as follows:

> The British Government representative said Martin Mc-Guinness' address to the Sinn Féin Ard Fheis 1993 had been read and triggered government action, Mayhew had

tried marginalisation. Defeating the IRA etc. That's gone. Coleraine speech was a significant move. (Mayhew had said that the British government had no strategic or selfish interest in Ireland.) Mayhew is now determined. He wants Sinn Féin to play a part not because he likes Sinn Féin but because it cannot work without them. Any settlement not involving all of the people North and South won't work. A North/South settlement that won't frighten unionists. The final solution is union. It is going to happen anyway. The historical train – Europe – determines that. We are committed to Europe. Unionists will have to change. This island will be as one.

He outlined the situation of talks at the level of delegations. The politicians, he said, were moving. The opportunity must be grasped. Next week if possible. British government is sincere. No cheating involved. He mentioned the [Merlyn] Rees letter to [Harold] Wilson: 'we set out to con them and we did'. The two weeks for talks proposed were repeated. He alleged that John Chilcott had instructed him to inform Sinn Féin that if this was agreed at six o'clock that clearance for meetings at the level of delegations would be forthcoming by one minute past six.

Confidentiality was of the utmost importance. Only Major, Mayhew, Hurd and secretary to the cabinet knew of all this. The British side would probably be led by Quentin Thomas with John Chilcott down the line. This issue of location for meetings was raised again.

Quentin Thomas did indeed lead negotiations with Martin Mc-Guinness and others for more than a year, but not the ones as outlined on that first night. The IRA did come back and offer a two-week (or more) ceasefire that would allow such contacts to take place, but that offer was not accepted.

12

Disappointment

ON THE NIGHT THAT THE IRA response to the beginning of negotiations with the British came back, Martin McGuinness arrived by himself. He came to the same room, Brendan Duddy's front office, where the initial meeting with Fred had taken place. Along with McGuinness there was only Duddy, Gallagher and me.

It was about ten days after the initial meeting. We were naturally hoping for a positive response to the request for a ceasefire to allow republicans to enter official discussions with the British, but hope is a long, long way from certainty.

McGuinness requested that someone take down a statement to the British government from Óglaigh na hÉireann (the Irish for Irish Republican Army). It took me a while to write it out because he dictated it, taking small, tightly scrunched-up pieces of paper from different parts of his clothing and speaking a few sentences at a time, drawing on what was contained on each little scrap of paper. I remember him looking at me on one occasion and saying, 'Don't you be changing any of this.' The statement contained the following: 'We are responding directly to your request for advice recognising fully the sensitivity of any position from you or us which is committed to paper at this stage. Our response has been couched accordingly but it is clear we are prepared to make the crucial move if a genuine peace process is set in place.'

By this time and after that last sentence, I was relieved and excited, as I am sure Duddy and Gallagher were, but everyone was acting in a restrained manner. The next few sentences were the clincher: 'You say that you require a private assurance in order to defend publicly your entry into dialogue with us … We wish now to proceed without delay to the delegation meetings. In order to facilitate this step, we sought and received a commitment which will permit you to proceed so that we can both explore the potential for developing a real peace process.'

There it was. The two-week ceasefire demanded to allow for talks to begin. At that stage I wanted to stand up, clench my fist and shout 'yes', the way golfers and winning football managers do. I didn't. I just smiled inwardly, and I think, although this might be retrospective and wishful thinking, I said a quiet prayer of thanksgiving.

I have read other versions of this statement that academics and Sinn Féin have published and there are very minor differences in some of the wording. But on that night what I was conscious of most was that I had come back into the backchannel with a belief that Martin McGuinness was committed to moving Irish republicans away from violence and into political dialogue with their avowed enemy and by extension with the other political parties, especially the unionist parties of the North. My instinct was that he had the ability and the stature to do that and that he could deliver. Here he was reading an official statement from the IRA confirming that indeed that is what he had intended and what he had achieved.

Strangely, there was a tension in the room that night and it was not just the seriousness of the message. It often happens that the import of an occasion can be displaced by a less pressing but more current worry. That was the case on a night when the three of us who had spent so much time in this house over the many years, discussing and arguing and planning and plotting, should have been overjoyed. And yet ...

A few days earlier Duddy had said to me that he thought he was in danger from the IRA. This was not the first time Duddy had felt under threat. He had expressed the fear before. I had never taken it all that seriously, in that I understood the tension and the anxiety that he felt. It would have been impossible to be in the position that he had created for himself without tension and stress. Sometimes I was his listening ear and sometimes I was irritated by unlikely theories and projections.

Duddy had fallen under the spell of the Maudsley/Rice training conferences. These were simulated training groups in societal behaviour. They were mostly targeted at those who had leadership ambitions in society, business or politics. The conferences, which took place over four or five days, explored the emotional relationship and interaction between an individual and a group. I had attended one in Dublin under the direction of the well-known Irish psychiatrist Garrett O'Connor, who became the director of the Betty Ford addiction centre in California. I had found the experience useful. Duddy, however, was fascinated by the process and became friendly with some of its practitioners in London. He participated in several such conferences, including some in Israel. He may, indeed, have acted as a facilitator on a few of them. I understood the attraction and was sympathetic to the emotional charge that the process provided, but I never thought him to be the most suitable person to attach himself to the process and I had tried on a few occasions to tell him that. My opinion was that his temperament and personality were too needy, and the conferences generated an amount of stress that was neither physically or psychologically healthy for him and was going to make him feel more threatened and fearful at times. Those warnings were not warmly received and never heeded.

Duddy, however, was the one in the spotlight. He was the one who mostly met the British. The relationship he had with the British was historical, including negotiating the 1975 six-month ceasefire that most of the present leadership of the IRA considered as having brought the movement to near defeat. On top of that, Duddy knew that McGuinness was no admirer or defender of his. So, while I considered Duddy to be overly sensitive to danger, I had an appreciation for his nervousness.

As McGuinness was leaving after dictating the offer of a ceasefire and discussions, I followed him and thanked him for his efforts in delivering the ceasefire. I took the opportunity to say that Duddy was feeling very pressured and threatened, that he felt he would be blamed if anything went wrong. I said that it was probably the intensity and the fragility of the issue and the burden of responsibility but added that I would like to reassure him that he was under no threat or danger from republicans. The response I got was not exactly warm and wholesome. Duddy was still not McGuinness' favourite person, but he gave me enough for me to be able to reassure Duddy that he was under no threat and that there was no danger to his life.

If Duddy was tense on that night, it would be true to say that I was tense during the next few weeks. Not because anyone or any organisation was threatening me, but because of the import of the messages that had been requested, responded to and were now awaiting follow-through.

Brendan Duddy's papers imply that the statement McGuinness dictated, and I wrote out by hand, was typed up in his office. He says that he never gave the statement to his British contacts but read it to them, and that their haste to get out of the room to relay the offer of the ceasefire to their political masters was almost unseemly. In their excitement, he claims, their manner was 'thank you, but could you see yourself to the door'. But irrespective of the speed of delivery, their political masters were much less excited and more cautious and negative than one would have expected or hoped for.

I had informed my family that there was a strong possibility that a week of negotiations between the IRA and the British was going to happen, probably in Scotland but that Norway had also been mentioned, and while there was no formal arrangement for Gallagher, Duddy and me to attend, the likelihood of us attending in the capacity of brokers and interlocutors had been mentioned. Apart from the concern about being adequate and competent in such a role, I had also never flown in a helicopter and had no desire to do so. A flight to Scotland in the dreaded helicopter was not to be welcomed; one to Norway would have been a nightmare.

But the days passed and the helicopter never came. Other dynamics and pressures were at play here. John Major had a slim majority in parliament. Those were the days of a precarious prime minister, the Maastricht Treaty negotiations and nine Ulster Unionist Party (UUP) votes controlled by James Molyneaux, the leader of the UUP in the House of Commons. A coterie of backbenchers was known for its opposition to closer ties between the EU and Britain, and was equally antagonistic about the possibility of any contact or negotiation with Irish republicans. It had the numbers to make life difficult for Major and to bring down the government. Indeed, Major had recently won a vote on Maastricht by a majority of just three as dozens of Conservative backbenchers voted against the government. As a result of this situation, the next few months would be very messy, but, disappointing and frustrating as it was, that night could not be scrubbed out. A line had been crossed and eighteen years after the first encounters between the two main antagonists, there would be no simple or sustainable return to where either of them had been.

The delay in responding to the offer of an IRA ceasefire obviously arose from the tensions and the differences within the Conservative Party. It was looking, once again, as if Ireland's needs were coming a very poor second to those of the internal needs of the British government. Eventually a response did come, in a request for a meeting with the backchannel. Normally Duddy attended such meetings on his own but, given the importance and the tensions, he wanted Gallagher and me to go with him. I agreed, but Gallagher, sensing the possible content of the meeting, decided against attending.

The venue was a back room in a hotel outside Antrim town, with John Deverall and Fred attending for the British. We were regaled with stories of the political difficulties faced by the prime minister and the government, and there was an amount of pleading for us to appreciate the complexity and subtlety of entering negotiations, while hoping that we could assure republicans that the paper which they were going to give to us to pass on to the

IRA meant that no windows or doors were being closed. They stressed that further talks would refine the parameters of future negotiations and that the good work that had led to the present moment would continue and lead to the type of result that we all wanted.

It probably wasn't as awful as my recollection might suggest, but observing the passing up or the letting drop of such an historic opportunity is always disappointing and deflating. We were being burdened with the job of delivering a rejection to the offer of a ceasefire and negotiations that had the strong potential to evolve into a permanent cessation of violence. This would obviously put the backchannel in jeopardy. The IRA was naturally going to consider the non-committal, even evasive response to their offer as a rejection and that was not going to sit well with those within the Army Council who had argued for moving away from violence, nor indeed with those who undoubtedly argued that it was unwise to trust the British.

It was unnerving for Duddy. Because he had already been feeling under pressure and even suspicion, this rejection was going to ratchet up those feelings. I later read somewhere that he had noted how during that phase of the negotiations the republican movement had put all their cards on the table, including the deeds of their house, and they hadn't even had the courtesy of a reply. This wasn't quite accurate because the reply became the issue. It formed the core of a hostile interrogation that took place in the upper sitting room of Duddy's house. McGuinness, Gerry Adams, Pat Doherty, Duddy and I were present. I can't remember if Gallagher was there. The meeting had a hostile atmosphere and lasted a few hours. The core of the interrogation was about why Duddy had gone to the meeting at the Antrim hotel and why he had accepted the written reply from Deverall and Fred. I was being given a fool's pardon – the same questions were not being directed at me.

I remained quiet for a time before interrupting and insisting that I was completely confused and unclear as to the purpose and the premise of the questions. I was not putting this on. I said so to Adams. Whether Duddy and I had gone to the meeting was irrelevant, I argued. The British would have delivered the response even if we hadn't gone to the meeting. They could have sent it by post or dropped it into the letterbox of Duddy's house or even my house. I didn't want to make matters worse for Duddy, so I restrained myself from saying that it was wrong and misplaced to vent their own disappointment and anger on the backchannel and especially on Duddy. Shooting the messenger stuff.

Whatever about the content, this meeting was signalling that the backchannel was coming to an end. It had survived many disappointments, but it was not going to survive this one.

Duddy was greatly shaken and even frightened by that meeting. He gauged it to be an interrogation of him personally, rather than an exploration of why the British had engaged and then reneged. I thought it was a very rough meeting and, in its tone and questioning, unfair and antagonistic to Duddy, but I didn't regard it as a threat to him. I saw it as the predictable and natural result of the strain that this group of men felt themselves to be under. They had pushed the boat far out from the harbour of violently fighting the war against the British and were now entering a different harbour that was less familiar and which carried with it its own set of dangers. It didn't take a genius to conclude that there would be sceptics and dissenters within the republican leadership, a fact confirmed by the realisation that this was only about the third time that Adams had turned up at a meeting with the backchannel.

However, I saw this as progress. Since the 1980s and up to the previous few weeks, McGuinness had been the sole contact. Now we had McGuinness, Kelly, Doherty and Adams, all within a short period. It had only been two years since McGuinness had first talked to me about republicans becoming peacemakers, and while the British had returned with a negative response to a substantial offer, this difficult meeting with a representation of the leadership could also be read as real progress on a road that was always going to be bumpy. And it might be one of the oldest clichés, but if this door was closing, it was doing so having delivered a key that others could use to open other doors.

To be sure that the impetus into politics would continue, it was clear that the backchannel needed to come to an end. The British government and the Conservative Party might have their needs, but they were nowhere near the needs of the people on the island of Ireland. The IRA had offered a ceasefire that the British had quibbled about and finally turned down. That was too important to be left in the secret caverns of a backchannel that allowed politicians and governments to pick and choose what suited them rather than the greater societal needs. The situation was calling out for a big hitter who could take this piece of information and use it to frame the dilemmas and the blockages in a broader, and indeed international, context. The Irish and the American governments should surely know and utilise such information to pressure both sides, most especially the British, into accepting the need for engagement and negotiation with militant republicanism, as well as with mainstream political parties. It was also becoming clear that the time had come for the backchannel to acknowledge its limitations and allow someone with the proper contacts and respect in Ireland and America, not forgetting Europe, to take matters to the next level by engaging the interest and the influence of these other governments. Fortunately, Albert Reynolds had unexpectedly become taoiseach of Ireland and, of course, there was John Hume, who lived just a few hundred yards down the street.

13

Driving the Peace Process Forward

JOHN HUME HAD BEEN MY history teacher in St Columb's College for two of the five years I was there from 1959 to 1964. In the first year his class was one of the few I looked forward to attending. There were two reasons for that. The first was that you knew that there was not going to be any corporal punishment – being slapped on the hands with a thick leather strap – as happened in those years. The second reason was that the three-quarter-hour lesson had a strong possibility of being interesting, particularly when Hume would challenge us to discuss and even debate for and against contentious issues, such as the case for nationalists to join the UUP to change its policies towards Catholics from within. The pros and cons of the European Union was another interesting subject for discussion and debate. Unfortunately, there was a set curriculum to be got through, mostly in English history, and we had exams at the end of the year, so not all classes were as stimulating as they might otherwise have been.

The discussions and the debates were much less frequent in the second year. Even as gauche teenagers we knew that there was a change, that our favourite teacher had not the same energy or interest as before. Some days you could see the tiredness in his face and if you didn't notice it in the face, you were certain to observe and hear the yawns. The class came to know that he had become active in the Credit Union movement, and he may have travelled far down the country and back the night before to address some event. The more astute students knew that he was not going to stay much longer in teaching. But at least we got the best of him in that first year.

Hume's house was not far from the cathedral, and in the short period that I was attached to that parish, he and I would have run into each other reasonably often. When I was sent to the Long Tower parish, I saw him less often. I hadn't anticipated and was surprised that he was so antagonistic to the establishment of the Bogside Community Association, and I was a bit annoyed that he allowed or encouraged one of his chief henchmen to come to tell me that I would be irresponsible to establish the organisation. In my later dealings with him, however, I had almost forgotten the issue; we never discussed it and I am sure it was the last thing on Hume's mind, especially considering how nervous he became around elections. I remember going into his office one day close to an election and him genuinely and nervously asking me how I thought he would do. This was at a time when Hume was attracting a vote that was out of sight of any of his opponents. That surprised me at the time, but the more contact I had with politicians, the more I realised the insecurity and vulnerability most of them felt.

We had another small spat one night in a hotel in the late

1970s. I had become quite friendly with some SDLP councillors and officials. On this night I was with Billy McCartney, a local businessman, a long-time donor and member of the local party and a strong supporter of Hume's. There had been the usual political discussion and argument over a few drinks, which continued into the foyer as McCartney, Hume and I were leaving. It became a little heated and Hume, in disagreeing with something I said about the need to talk to republicans, called me 'a Provo priest' – it would have been known within the locality that McGuinness and I spoke reasonably often. But I didn't have to defend myself on that occasion because McCartney scolded Hume for the unfairness and the inaccuracy of his remark. Hume took the scolding very well.

I had played no part in organising the first meeting between Hume and the IRA, but I drove him part of the way to that meeting. This was during the time I had stopped going to meetings with Duddy and Gallagher but hadn't lost contact with them. I was a bit surprised but delighted when Duddy told me that Hume was going to meet with the IRA and asked me to drive him across the border into Donegal. That was back in 1985, five or more years before more substantial meetings between Hume and republicans took place. It came about because of a remark Hume made on television that Sinn Féin were only surrogates for the IRA and that if he was going to talk to anyone it would only be to the people who gave the orders and not those who only took the orders. This led to the Army Council challenging Hume to meet with some of its members.

I don't remember why it was necessary for me to drive Hume across the border only to meet up with Duddy, who then drove him to somewhere outside Letterkenny where he was transferred to a van and driven around for a few hours before alighting at a house where he was to meet and talk with three members of the IRA. I do remember coming back to Derry and visiting Hume's wife, Pat. I called with her a few times over the next few days. It was easy to appreciate the bravery of Hume in allowing himself to be driven off into the unknown and to appreciate the worry and strain it put on Pat, who was sitting at home not knowing where he was, how he was and I am sure, in her worst moments, wondering if he would come back home alive.

He did. But only after a fruitless encounter. The IRA insisted that the discussions with him should be videoed. Hume, naturally and rightly, insisted that no such thing was going to happen. The stand-off was not resolved, and Hume arrived home. He had been away for three days. The raising and the dashing of hopes was becoming too commonplace.

Around the time of the negative response from the British government to the ceasefire offered by the IRA, followed by that fraught meeting with Adams, McGuinness and Doherty, we took the time to scrutinise the role of the backchannel. The three of us who had been involved took an afternoon to talk to each other about the future and our part in it.

It was becoming unhealthy to allow the two main combatants in the thirty-year conflict to attend to their own internal political issues without due regard to for resolution and for peace. John Major and his senior ministers turning their face against an opportunity to explore and facilitate dialogue rather than conflict was only the most recent example of this.

It was time to expose these realities and these questions to the light and to public scrutiny. That could not be done by any of the three people involved in the backchannel sitting around the table. It would need to be done by a major public figure. Hume was the obvious and correct person for the job. His standing in Ireland coupled with his reputation in America gave him the type of access and status that was needed. Inviting Hume to meet and briefing him fully on the level and length of contact between the British and the IRA would be the end of the backchannel. It had been built on confidentiality and trust, with both sides assured that the contact and the messages delivered between them would be outside of the public gaze. Revealing these to Hume, or to any politician other than one from Sinn Féin, would be seen as a breach of these conditions by the IRA, while disclosing to him that the IRA had offered a ceasefire, which had been rejected, would be regarded as a breach by the British government.

But the backchannel was in danger of becoming an obstacle to the goal it wished to achieve. It had been established to bring two sides into negotiation with each other and it now appeared to be allowing them both to luxuriate in having a secret liaison while maintaining an opposite public position. On the other hand there was the danger that, out of frustration and pique, we were destroying the line of communication when there were signs of engagement, despite recent disappointments.

I remember Duddy warning that if we briefed Hume fully and if the knowledge that we shared with him led to a positive outcome of dialogue and negotiations between the British and the IRA, we should expect to be cast aside and ignored. Politics was like that and the years of work that had been done to bring the British to the realisation that they had to talk to the IRA and the equal years spent providing the IRA with the means and the mechanism to engage with the British might receive a glancing nod but little more than that. I agreed that that was the likely outcome but that it should not stop us from doing the right thing.

'Are you in this too?' was Hume's greeting to me as I walked into Duddy's house a few days later. During the next few hours Duddy, Gallagher and I briefed him fully and told him everything. We revealed the extent and the longevity of the contacts between the British government and the IRA that had been initiated and facilitated by the backchannel, and the type and volume of messages that had flowed through that channel over the years. For authentication purposes, Duddy told him a few things that Hume had discussed with secretaries of state and that could only have been known to senior officials within the NIO and those they chose to share them with, the backchannel being one such group. We showed him a copy of the Hume–Adams document. We brought him up to date with the events of the last few weeks and the rejection by the British of the ceasefire offer. We advised that he should do what he considered best with this information but suggested that he should choose carefully the people he might share it with, those with the ability to challenge and even embarrass the British government.

As is well documented, Hume was under enormous pressure at the time. His party was restless and fearful that he was taking a wrong road. A few weeks before this meeting, Adams had been seen coming out of Hume's house and this had been reported in the media, piling on more pressure. Some journalists, especially some in the Southern Irish media, were negative and hostile to his efforts to engage with Adams and Sinn Féin. So, what he was being told on that night was akin to a water hydrant being supplied to a dehydrated man in a very large and hostile desert.

Years later I was told by a television producer that Gerry Adams had said that I was mistaken in claiming that Hume was unaware of the contact between the British and the IRA. I would strongly assert that on the night we filled Hume in on the extent and the duration of the contact, he was greatly surprised and greatly relieved. He now had material that a good politician could use to make and advance his case.

After that night, if it hadn't been clear before, it certainly was clear now that the backchannel had reached its end. The only question was whether to tell Sinn Féin that we had informed Hume of the contacts and the offer from the IRA of a ceasefire. We decided to do so.

I remember meeting McGuinness in the Long Tower parochial house – I was still playing the 'priest' card. The administrator of the parish, Fr Michael Collins, was a close friend and very protective of me. He had no great interest in politics and never interrogated what I was doing but trusted that it was for the good. I had the run of the parochial house. I thought this might be a difficult meeting, as did Duddy and Gallagher, so it was best that it took place in a setting which might be more restrictive to raising voices beyond acceptable levels. However, the meeting was somewhat of an anticlimax. Maybe he expected it, maybe he wanted it that way, but when I outlined to McGuinness what had happened and the extent to which we had briefed Hume, he shrugged his shoulders and said something like, 'Okay.' He was so laid back about it that I was surprised.

There were now a lot of balls flying in the air. The only thing that was clear was that, with the backchannel past its sell-by date, matters had to move on to a different and more public position. To keep anything secret or private in the political or, more accurately, semi-political world was difficult. The fact that the backchannel had remained a secret for so many years was somewhat miraculous. Now that Hume was fully briefed and that its existence was moving into the political world, the likelihood of it remaining secret was reducing. So, it surprised me that Sinn Féin decided that they wanted it to continue.

Out of the blue one day, about a fortnight after I had told him about briefing John Hume, McGuinness arrived at my home with an envelope. He told me that the personnel in the backchannel – Duddy, Gallagher and I – were to be replaced with the people whose names were contained in the letter in the envelope. Would I ensure that the letter was delivered to the government? I can't remember if McGuinness was conscious of the irony of that request, but I am sure he knew that I would want to know who our replacements were. Even though the letter was being handed to me, the person who was really being sacked was Duddy.

McGuinness had scarcely left the house before Noel Gallagher arrived. The opening of the envelope revealed to us two people we both knew. It wasn't my business to enquire if these people had been asked to do the job, or how much or little about the original backchannel they knew. There was much that could have been discussed, but the atmosphere around being sacked was not conducive to a long discussion. It was better to leave any arguments to another day. I don't think the names were ever delivered to the British and the two named people are long dead. And as often happened at the time, events intervened, with a report on Sunday, 28 November 1993 in *The Observer* under the headline 'Major's secret links with IRA leadership revealed' blowing the lid off all the secrecy:

Exclusive: Whitehall uses 'hero' go-betweens to set up contacts with men of violence – Peace feelers out since 1989

A secret communication chain has been running between the Government and the IRA with the Prime Minister's approval, an authoritative British source has told *The Observer*.

The contacts have been in place for many months. Confirming that there had been contacts, the Northern Ireland Office said in a statement to *The Observer* last night: 'The IRA have not delivered the ending of violence envisaged in their original approach.

'They have continued to inflict untold misery and grief upon the public. It is for them to explain this. There can be no excuse for such terrorism. Their duty is to end it at once.'

Later, in an attempt to limit the impact of today's exclusive *Observer* report on the text of one messenger's aide memoire, Whitehall said the IRA leadership had sent a message to the Government in February, to the effect that 'conflict was over, but they needed our advice as to the means of bringing it to a close'.

'The Government obviously had to take that message seriously, though we recognised that actions, not words, would be the real test.'

The communication link was said by the source to be a message-delivery service run by unofficial intermediaries; deniable 'heroes' who began operating after British Ministers' public overtures – going back as far as 1989 – brought a positive reaction from the IRA.

The process, so secret that it was not even disclosed by

John Major to Albert Reynolds, the Irish Prime Minister, was described as an essential response to the terrorists' 'peace feelers'.

The go-betweens included clergymen, professionals and businessmen. The *Observer* source said that messengers often put their own lives at risk. Although the source emphatically denied direct government involvement, Sinn Féin chief of staff Martin McGuinness and others have said that a civil servant was used.

In a separate development, Mr McGuinness tells BBC TV's *On the Record* today: 'John Major knows who the contact is.' He claimed meetings had sometimes taken place daily, and were continuing. According to *The Observer*'s information, the chain of contacts led to a key meeting with Mr McGuinness just after the Warrington bombing on 20 March, when both sides exchanged formal 'position' papers.

According to Dublin sources, a further meeting was planned at which each side would be represented by four 'negotiators'. It was to take place outside Ireland – possibly abroad. Britain was said to have pressed hard for it to take place at Easter, but said that it would be conditional on a two-week ceasefire by the IRA.

The long-delayed official admission of contacts, sanctioned by Sir Patrick Mayhew, Northern Ireland Secretary, will put peace on a knife-edge in the run-up to Friday's Anglo-Irish summit.

I am very uncertain of the chronology and the source of the revelation of the backchannel. It didn't surprise me that it was leaked, but rumours about the source and the rationale for the leak were confusing. A question in the House of Commons from the Labour MP Dennis Skinner on 1 November to the Prime Minister John Major indicated he had some inkling of the contact. Major's answer at the time had been that it would turn his stomach if he had to talk to Adams and republicans. A story coming back to Duddy, Gallagher and me was that it was someone within the Democratic Unionist Party (DUP) who was the source of the leak. But how did they get hold of it in the first place? That only led to further speculation that the government itself had leaked, to test public and political reaction. It certainly came at a time when McGuinness and Sinn Féin were pushing forward with the proposition that they wanted to bring about peace and that the blockage was coming from the British side.

Whatever about the sequencing and the source of the revelation, the image in my head is McGuinness arriving at my home of a morning. It was clear that he was under pressure. He hadn't time to fill me in on all the details, he had others to meet with shortly, but he wanted me to do a press conference, probably that afternoon. He wanted me to confirm that the backchannel had been in place for years, that messages had flown through that channel way back into the 1970s, that it was very active during the years of the hunger strikes and had recently facilitated talks and an offer of a ceasefire from the IRA.

I remember visualising the outcome of sitting beside Mc-Guinness at a press conference and speaking of such sensitive issues. The press conference itself didn't scare me, but I knew the consequences would be horrendous. I had been a semi-public person for years, but this would project me, for a time, onto a different level. But worst of all, it would have consequences for my family. They would be drawn into a public arena that I had managed to spare them from up to now.

I envisaged all that, but I still agreed to do the press conference. McGuinness had shared with me his intention of changing the focus of republicanism from violence to politics and I had been close enough to observe those efforts coming to greater coherence, even if they had quite a distance to travel. He had indulged me on a few important occasions in pushing him a little bit further than he might have been comfortable with. Without telling me what was happening within the organisation and without telling me the depth of the pressure that he was feeling, his request to do the press conference was a definite plea for help and I felt he had earned that from me. Then, three or so hours later, he arrived back at my house to say that he (or they) had decided against the press conference. He appeared less strained, if still agitated. Things were happening fast and bursting out into the open.

It wasn't just McGuinness who reacted nervously to *The Observer*'s revelations. John Chilcot, the chief of the NIO, gave an interview before he died claiming that, from his perspective, matters came to a head on the Monday morning after the story broke. He described sitting in the House of Commons fearful of the backlash he expected to come from members of parliament. However, what he actually witnessed was a general welcoming that the government was in dialogue and trying to resolve the conflict. He portrayed it as a wonderful moment.

Maybe it was a case of when it seems that things are falling apart, they are falling into place. The premise that the two most ruthless combatants had to liaise and negotiate with each other was becoming more prominent and acceptable. John Hume was now well briefed and was busy pulling in behind his efforts his many contacts in America and in Europe. While the initial expectation was that Taoiseach Albert Reynolds would have little interest in the affairs of Northern Ireland, it turned out that his priority was to bring the North to the centre of attention for the Irish government and to challenge the British government to become more engaged than previously. He was displaying an energy and a resolve that former taoisigh had lacked.

Despite the surprising positivity of the members of the House of Commons, as observed by John Chilcot, and my analysis that matters might be falling together rather than apart, the coming months and even years were messy. Messy in that Adams and McGuinness and others had to coax, cajole, steer and guide the republican movement away from violence and into politics. They had to do that against the backdrop of a British prime minister who also had to coax and cajole his government and his country around to the idea that republicans had to be included in negotiated attempts to construct a package that would end the war and allow inclusive politics to take its place. The terminus was clear, the journey towards it was erratic – stop, start, inch by inch. These were long and painful months for John Hume, when he was subjected to the caution and the self-protection of the two main combatants of the long and dirty war. From what I observed, both were more caring to the needs of their own party or organisation and far from properly sensitive to his needs.

Hume was left in limbo for months, sidelined from the decisions both antagonists had to make and with too much thinking and worrying time on his hands. He routinely visited certain houses where he might receive some comfort or pick up some information that might change the bleakness of his situation. One of those houses was mine. He would spend a few hours, smoking cigarettes and drinking coffee. The conversation was repetitive. He would ask what I thought he should do, and I would say that I thought he should go public in demanding an immediate ceasefire from the IRA and a guarantee from the government that Sinn Féin would be included in negotiations immediately. His response was always that he was afraid of pushing the IRA too hard and losing the momentum towards peace that he was certain was building up. My response was that they were ready to make peace, but they needed to be pushed and that he was the one in the strongest position to do the pushing.

In that limbo, he felt that he could not fully address the concerns and the suspicions of his own political party, fearful he might betray confidences and insights that might allow one or other of the combatants to walk away from the decisions that had to be made. The silence was heightening the tensions and fears within his own party that he had taken a wrong turn, that he had made a mistake in talking to Adams and co., that he was going to lose the confidence and the trust of the membership. He was also taking a battering from the media, most especially the Southern Irish media, who were accusing him of giving succour to the IRA rather than to those who had become victims because of the actions and the ruthlessness of the IRA.

That December, an hour-long private meeting in Dublin Castle between Reynolds and Major took place, the one after which Reynolds told Irish officials, 'It went all right – I chewed his bollocks off, and he took a few lumps outa me.' The 'bollocking' was no doubt about the deception of the British in keeping the knowledge of the backchannel to themselves and even worse, hiding from the Irish the depth of the contacts between the British and the IRA and, unforgivably, the offer of a ceasefire that the British had rejected.

The Irish government was on the front foot and Reynolds used it to bring about the Downing Street Declaration. It was launched in London just two weeks after that famous meeting in Dublin Castle. The declaration was the first time that the British government formally recognised a right of self-determination for the 'people of the island of Ireland'. Reynolds had only a short time as taoiseach, but when it came to Anglo-Irish matters, and to Northern Ireland and the disbandment of the IRA, he used that time well. It wasn't only the British he confronted and pushed further down the road of negotiation. Gallagher informed me that he had also softened up Adams, McGuinness and others in the republican movement with a few 'bollockings'. He made the job of driving the peace process forward much easier for those who followed him.

There was no role now for any 'link' or 'backchannel'. Most matters were out in the open and the issues had moved into the political mainstream. However, there was one last input from Duddy, Gallagher and myself, and for some reason it is one of only a few pieces of paper relating to the years of the peace process that I have in my possession. It is dated to 16 November 1994, agreed between the three of us in the backchannel, and it clearly came in that frustrating time when proposed talks were on and then off, subjected to a demand or a red line from one side or the other. The IRA had finally called their ceasefire the previous year, but questions of permanence or decommissioning became the stumbling blocks. Sinn Féin had not yet sat down in a structured, formal way forward with the British government,

Peace Comes Dropping Slow

although it was being suggested that a series of such talks should take place. The document I have is a letter that I delivered to McGuinness and is self-explanatory:

The primary task of the present British government is to remain in office until June 1997. From Sinn Féin's public statements, you are well aware of this.

A genuine settlement in Ireland, i.e. a settlement acceptable to the Irish people, would be used as an excuse by the Tory Party to oust John Major. But more importantly, John Major is a unionist. At two vital moments, on the eve of the last general election in 1992 and on the eve of this year's Tory conference, John Major spoke not on the economy or on Europe but rather on the Labour Party's threat to break the Union between Scotland and England. We also know that you know this.

John Major's cabinet and the NIO are creating a position in which Sinn Féin have to be the reactors. The British are very good at this, they have a long history of putting their opponents at a disadvantage.

The frontal approach will be one of making progress, but the main objective will be to disadvantage the republican movement. The main progress carrot is Major's and Mayhew's constant referral to the British Government's intention to hold talks with the Republican Movement before Christmas. This is what Sinn Féin has been asking for, for years. This is what the nations of the world are saying is right to happen etc.

Our advice is: DON'T GO! UNLESS

Unless the Framework Document is published.

If you enter talks before the Framework Document is published the British Government will be in control of the drip, drip, drip. Sinn Féin will be forced to complain about the slow progress and the real core issues not being discussed. Sinn Féin will appear to be the negative complaining party and the British Government will appear eminently reasonable. The Framework Document will show in which direction and how far the British Administration is prepared to travel. It is a much better political strategy to switch tactics and put the British on the defensive. The British are leaking through the media that the current crisis in the South will inevitably delay the Framework Document; this creates the opportunity to switch tactics.

Remember. The British do not want this cessation to break down, neither do they wish to do serious business with Sinn Féin. It has always been our advice that the British will have to be moved along the peace process on a step-by-step basis.

Finally, Sinn Féin must announce this policy before the British announce the date for the talks. (Our contention is that the talks will be announced very soon, before the end of November.) If you accept this analysis, Sinn Féin's announcement and follow-up interviews can be done in a most reasonable and temperate manner, not in a strident, defensive manner.

If you wish further clarification on this proposal – You know where we live.

Apart from the very poor writing and the cringeworthy ending, it is an interesting letter. The Framework Document was an extensive outlining of the principal divisions existing in Northern Ireland, the parameters and approaches to which both the British and Irish governments agreed in order to address these divisions and bring an end to violence. (It was the blueprint for the Good Friday Agreement.) I wrongly thought that there was a suggestion in the letter that Sinn Féin should not, initially, attend the talks but should ask Hume and the SDLP to substitute for them for a time. I do remember proposing that to McGuinness outside his house on the night I delivered the letter. I also remember thinking that that proposal was not going to get an innings when there were mutterings from him that he didn't think too many in his party would buy the suggestion.

Sinn Féin entered the talks. McGuinness led on behalf of the party and Quentin Thomas, who was political director at the NIO, led for the British. The talks lasted for over a year before the Canary Warf bomb exploded in London, killing three people, setting the peace process back for a time and leading to Sinn Féin being excluded from the talks for a while.

I was on my way to the cinema when I heard that a bomb had exploded in London. The film was *Heat* with Al Pacino and Robert de Niro. On that night, it did not succeed in holding my attention or lifting my depressed mood, and I have never been able to sit and watch the film without associating it with Quentin Thomas, who became the president of the British Board of Film Classification, the film censor, after he retired from his position in politics. In more recent times he gave an interview to Niall Ó Dochartaigh, who curated Brendan Duddy's papers. In it, he said:

Where I have some sympathy with them [Sinn Féin] is that there was a sort of line from outside, 'If you only renounce violence we'll be imaginative, you'll be surprised how imaginative we are.' But actually, when they did make their, what for them was a major historical statement, we said, 'Well actually I'm not sure you mean it. You haven't quite said, you haven't used the word permanent, have you?' We were quite niggling about it, whereas we implied that we were going to be frightfully imaginative ... when they made their statement in August '94 I think it was our side started to quibble about the terms. Now we were not wrong to do that because it wasn't absolutely clear and subsequent events showed that it wasn't clear because we had a bomb in Canary Wharf and so on. But we then got ourselves in a position of saying, 'Well, of course if you really mean it, the best way you can demonstrate that is give up your arms' ... it's not a wrong position but it was kind of, I suppose the word I'd use, it was a bit clumsy. Because it then became this thing that became central to the process, but one couldn't get around it ... And the Unionists too were sucked in because I remember when Trimble was elected and he was asked about this, he said quite rightly, 'Well this is not my point, this is the British government who have been going on about this, go and talk to them about it.' But, of course, he couldn't sustain that. In the end he had to make it his own as well. He had to become one of the principal proponents of the view that arms had to be given up ... the talks from '96 to '98 were bedevilled by this issue. It was the thing we had to get around the whole time and of course it continued for long after the Good Friday Agreement. And I think that was not very clever; actually, it was rather clumsy.

Clumsy is a good word to capture the British government's attitude and approach to the peace process. That statement from Thomas is honest and revealing, up to a point. It talks of his side promising an imaginative response but not delivering on that promise. It admits to being obtrusive and miserly rather than expansive and encouraging. A close examination of the talks and a reading of Thomas' and others' insights into them confirms those negative reactions, but a civil servant of his stature knows only too well that the party who controls the reins of government will ultimately control the tenor and ambience of such talks. The Conservatives were split and in possession of a small and unstable majority. That is why the talks were so long-drawn-out and clumsy. The letter given to McGuinness advising him not to go into those talks until the Framework Document was published was correct in its assessment and predictions.

Unfortunately, Sinn Féin and its membership were also looking to manage the tensions within its ranks. There were already rumblings within the IRA from those who would eventually split off to form the Real IRA and that was before two of the more sensitive and difficult issues – decommissioning of arms and policing – came onto the table. But there would be no avoiding those issues; they were coming down the road and onto everyone's plate.

14

A Seemingly Impossible Vision

WITH THE PASSING OF THE backchannel, my involvement in the process changed. I became a political commentator and analyst, arguing and debating in public what I had previously raised only in private. But one of us who formed the backchannel refused to let go: Noel Gallagher.

For a long time, Gallagher's name and his influence were known only to a few, so when the peace process was being discussed or analysed, he was seldom included or else there was a vague reference to a third man who was involved in the backchannel. I suppose he and I had become like brothers. One of my sisters has an expression: 'I love the kind of him.' I loved the kind of Gallagher. He was colourful in speech, unsophisticated and loyal. I always knew he had my back, as they say in Derry. But Gallagher was not always the easiest person to work with. He was given to exaggeration and obfuscation that bordered on the deceptive. He was disorganised and scattered to an extent that bordered on unreliable. Many people mistook his personality and his scattered approach as bumptiousness. Some of this may have prevented people in power from seeing behind the human foibles to the giftedness and intelligence that resided in the same person. In fact, I remember being asked by someone how I could have worked with such a paradoxical person. I replied that I could identify many foibles in myself and that I had observed plenty of foibles in people like Hume and McGuinness; that I took some delight and pride in the fact I was able to identify the gifts and the strengths in Gallagher that were of such importance.

Those strengths began with the fact that he had steeped himself in the republican tradition and had come to know, understand and interpret it better than anyone I had ever known. A born politician, he had an inherent, native intelligence, often expressed in wonderfully colourful and rich, if somewhat earthy, language. He also firmly believed in the political process and that republicans, if the conflict was ever to be resolved, needed to be more sophisticated in their politics than the British. He had spent years debating with the older generation of republicans, especially Ruairí Ó Brádaigh. He also spent lots of time arguing with, and maybe teaching, Martin McGuinness.

Many politicians would not have been able to work with someone like Gallagher and it was the greatest fortune that Albert Reynolds, Bertie Ahern and Brian Cowen succeeded each other within Fianna Fáil and as taoisigh. They were all men who had their own foibles and yet they were all men who fell under the peculiar spell of Gallagher.

I don't know when Gallagher first met Albert Reynolds, but I have an indistinct memory of Gallagher and Brendan Duddy telling me that they had met with him after an event in Derry and that they had briefed him for a few hours. My first meeting with

Reynolds was about Bloody Sunday rather than the peace efforts. I had asked him to meet some members of the Bloody Sunday families who had some concerns about what was happening in their efforts to have the Widgery Tribunal overthrown and a new tribunal established. I must have asked Gallagher to set up the meeting and Reynolds must still have been minister for finance at the time because I remember him arriving at my house without ceremony or pomp. Had he been taoiseach that would not have been possible. He came to the house, and I put him in a room with the families and he talked with them for a few hours.

Over time, Noel Gallagher's relationship with Albert Reynolds strengthened, and the two men became close friends. Gallagher was up and down the road to Dublin like a butterfly in those weeks and months when Reynolds was taoiseach, and he kept me well briefed on developments. His experience, knowledge and insight must have been a comfort and a spur to the taoiseach in his negotiations within the Anglo-Irish context.

However, the long hours that he spent on his involvement inevitably took their toll on both his business and his family. In an article I later wrote as a tribute to Gallagher, I recalled how 'I sometimes berated him for getting his priorities wrong. I accused him of being even more besotted with politics than I was. On occasions I stung him by pointing out that dedication to a "cause" may be motivated by altruism, but just as often it can be motivated by egotism. None of that stopped him; my words fell on deaf ears.' I suspect, in fact, that the time he spent on the political situation drove his business to near bankruptcy. I know I wrote a letter to Brian Cowen, and I think I wrote one to Bertie Ahern, asking that a formal role and position be found that would provide Gallagher with some income. I also once scolded

Martin McGuinness that, after he came to power in the Stormont Executive, he could have found a position for Gallagher on one of the many public bodies. He appointed several others to positions that Gallagher could easily have filled. I felt Gallagher was treated badly by those who had used him when needed and dropped him when the initial issues were resolved.

Gallagher received no formal or public recognition, and always made his contribution away from the public gaze. Indeed, when I wrote the abovementioned article, he was reluctant for his name to be used and it talks simply about 'the individual'. While it was certainly good for others to read how an ordinary person could have such an influence in bringing about change in an horrendous conflict, the absence of a name almost demoted this to an aspiration, a mission statement, and took some of the punch and interest from the article.

Perhaps Gallagher felt that there was reward enough in reaching goals within the peace process that he helped bring about. One of the most important of these was the long-awaited start to decommissioning in October 2001. This was a step that many felt would never be taken, but it was a vital issue that would dog the Good Friday Agreement until an agreement on it was reached. The IRA's absolute of 'not an ounce, not a bullet' had appeared unshakeable, and yet on 24 October that year the announcement came: 'In order to save the peace process we have implemented this scheme.' Comments from political leaders at the time show just how remarkable this announcement was. John Reid, the secretary of state for Northern Ireland, called it 'a seemingly impossible vision', while David Trimble said, 'This is the day we were told we would never see.'

It is hard to know what changed the republican movement's mind on this issue. At the time, it was suggested that mounting pressure, combined with the detention of three IRA men in Colombia in August 2001, who were later charged with arriving on false passports and training FARC rebels in bomb-making, and the tragedy of 11 September in America may have influenced the decision. However, while I believe such analyses were well informed and probably have some validity, they were looking at purely external events and failed to take into account the complex internal workings of the peace process and the interplay of personality on personality. As I noted in my article on Gallagher, 'The Republican Movement has a leadership cluster, as does the Irish Government, no more than four or five individuals in all. Pivotal to both these groups was the man I've been referring to. His knowledge, political acumen and vision constantly informed, reassured, cajoled and ultimately persuaded these people to deliver.'

I was sometimes witness to fraught phone calls and meetings. Gallagher's was a reassuring but determined voice, ready to convince first Reynolds and then Ahern and Cowen to hold their nerve; that a deal could be done and the republicans could deliver on their promises. Occasionally the arguments were reversed: 'Republicans have their difficulties too. They need more than they are being offered.' Sometimes a trip to Dublin was essential to remind the government that they too were republicans and couldn't walk away from the process just because the going got tough.

I finished my article on Gallagher with a summation that I feel can't be bettered here:

It's convenient, but misleading, almost, to represent such exchanges in a matter of sentences. It took weeks, months, years of dedication, persistence, integrity and above all foresight. People who can tell you what happened yesterday are two-a-penny; the person who can tell you what'll happen next month is priceless.

'Historic' is the adjective which has been used to describe the decommissioning of IRA arms. It is an apt description. History is defined as the continuous recording of events; the study of the past involving human affairs; the systematic or critical analysis of past events. Sometimes our understanding of history is largely one of sequencing: this happened, then this happened, and so on. Lost in that is the hugely important input of the subjective. More often than the tomes ever acknowledge, there's the influence and the centrality of the individual. If the events of the last week [the announcement of decommissioning] really do prove to be the endgame in the British–Irish conflict, then both these islands owe an enormous debt to this one individual. For the moment, though, his name must go unspoken. Such is history.

Before decommissioning took place I had written and spoken about how republicans, in fully entering the political arena, had no option but to decommission their weapons. However, not everyone agreed with this viewpoint. In one article I recalled the story of a man I met in my local bakery. He was around his early sixties and the radio in the background was droning on about decommissioning. This prompted him to say, 'I wouldn't give the bastards a single bullet.' Although his words were aimed at the radio, I could see that his anger was directed at me. He clearly didn't agree with some of the public statements I'd made on the divisive subject of disarmament, and he wasn't the only one. Friends of mine who were committed republicans let me know in no uncertain terms that they did not agree with me either, although, after some proper discussion and debate, a few were gracious enough to concede that I 'might have a point'.

The 'arms issue' was a real danger to the step-by-step development of alternatives to violence. I suggested in that same article that the then Irish Catholic Cardinal, Seán Brady, should lead a day of prayer as a prelude to an act of decommissioning of arms by the IRA. The premise was that an action that helps your own people was not an act of surrender – the concern that lay behind the deepest emotional and symbolic resistance to decommissioning.

At this time of heightened tension, a young woman who was married to Martin McGuinness' brother and who had been an active member of the youth club to which I had been chaplain, died. The expression in Derry is that 'it was a wake on me'. I had been on the radio that morning arguing for decommissioning and when I walked into the wake it was full of IRA members from all over the North. As the saying goes, you could have cut the atmosphere with a knife, but it was a wake, and no one was going to argue or be rude in those circumstances. But for a pinch of reassurance, I called with Gallagher to ensure that he was keeping the pressure on the Irish government in insisting that decommissioning had to take place in some format.

Surprisingly, when decommissioning finally happened, the Provos went further with it than I thought they would. *Metanoia* is a Greek word that is found in Christian theology. It describes a complete change of heart signified by a change in one's way of life resulting from penitence or spiritual conversion. It would be too much to expect any repentance from the republican movement, but the decision and the action of decommissioning weapons to convert to a political ambience was a profound and transformative change. It pushed the peace process to another level. It allowed the next big obstacle to be addressed: policing.

15

New Challenges

AT THIS STAGE I WAS in my own twilight world. Distanced from any involvement from what was going on, I saw McGuinness off and on, but increasingly off, as he became more and more busy with his own and Sinn Féin's developing talks and the slow but inevitable journey into the agreed political institutions. I also saw Duddy less often, but Gallagher more often than ever.

Relationships between Duddy and Gallagher were slowly souring. The reversal of roles was too great for the relationship to survive. Duddy had the inside track for years with the British government; Gallagher and I were advisers and supporters, just managing to hold Sinn Féin and the IRA back from breaking the precarious relationship with the backchannel. Gallagher was now on the inside track with the ear of the Irish government. It was not quite a reversal of roles, but it was easy enough to appreciate that Duddy was now redundant. The British were conducting their own engagement with republicans and the Irish had decided that Gallagher was their adviser.

To be fair to Duddy, he would have been wary and fearful of Gallagher's tendency for exaggeration and inconsistency. He approached me on a few occasions to advise me of these worries. My response was that the leading politicians of Ireland were well capable of reading Gallagher's eccentricities, but that he would not be too far out or mistaken when it came to the substantive issues.

If Duddy was redundant, I was even more so. As regards work or engagement with the Troubles, the only thing I can point to are the columns I began to write for *The Irish News*. I can't remember why I was asked to do these, but I do remember that I was reluctant, afraid even. I had no confidence that I could write. For most of the documents or policy statements concerning the House in the Wells, Northlands Centre and other organisations and issues I had engaged with over the years, I turned to my wife, Mary. I considered her a very good writer. She was direct and insightful and able to distil complex issues down to digestible portions.

I do remember that Malachi O'Doherty, a columnist and author himself, encouraged me to accept the invitation to write for *The Irish News*. He insisted that there is a small muscle in the brain that lies dormant but when tapped into and exercised, it allows for written self-expression. That image helped me get started.

But I must have been writing more than I remember and it is the things that I forget that often surprise me. For example, *The Tablet* magazine is rightly considered a prestigious Catholic publication with a worldwide readership. I discovered among the small number of papers that I kept, an article I had written on policing. I cannot remember when I wrote it, who asked me to write it or why. But the article is there on the page, my name is attached to it and the sentiments reflect what I thought at the time.

Even though I can't remember the genesis of the *Tablet* article, I have a clear memory of a journey to San Diego, California, with a group of people made up of opinion-makers and senior police officers from the RUC, some of whom were tasked with drawing up the implementation papers for the new policing service as outlined in the Patten Report. The invitation came from Mediation Northern Ireland, an organisation led by Brendan McAllister from Newry. Brendan had assembled a small group of academics and was quietly beavering away in the world of politics, analysing and promoting steps towards peace and re-conciliation. Mediation had established a trusting relationship with the hierarchy of the RUC and a good outreach to Sinn Féin and other political parties and was providing workshops and training in the new challenges for policing. The organisation laid a lot of the tarmac that the politicians and the police and even the Policing Board later walked on to allow the new Police Service of Northern Ireland (PSNI) to have a chance to survive and prosper in the early years of the changes outlined in the Patten Report. Brendan McAllister and his people received little enough recognition or appreciation for the invaluable work that they did. Sadly, as I reread this section during writing, word came through to me that Brendan had died of a heart attack. I was shocked and greatly saddened, as he was only in his sixties.

Mediation Northern Ireland had organised the week-long trip to San Diego. The purpose was to experience policing in a different country and in a different culture. The bulk of the participants were to be police officers from the RUC, some of whom were engaged in translating the recommendations contained in the Patten Report into practical, day-to-day policies. I was one of the civilian participants asked on the trip, to observe and analyse as an ordinary member of the public who had some interest in the politics and history of Ireland, North and South. I presume that they had heard me on the radio or had read some of the first articles I had written for *The Irish News*. As I wasn't doing much at the time, I agreed to go.

It was a memorable trip. San Diego is a beautiful city and a day trip across the border to Tijuana in northern Mexico provided a touch of the colour and wildness of that country. The days spent together in America provided me with an insight into the desire and willingness of the RUC 'change management' participants to introduce a new beginning to policing in Northern Ireland. The purpose of the trip was to allow the group to spend a week working with senior police officers in San Diego, examining the differences between the two distinct police departments and also examining what were the obstacles to bringing about change and renewal to such a service. The enthusiasm that the RUC members showed for Patten's recommendations, their willingness to acknowledge the difficulties involved and their understanding of what a difference such change, particularly the depoliticisation of policing, impressed me greatly. But mostly I was impressed by the people.

An interesting exercise was carried out during that week. We were asked to place ourselves in a line based on our belief in the possibility of change. The top indicated a 100 per cent belief that change could be achieved, the middle a 50 per cent belief, and so on. I placed myself on the negative end of the line, which did shock some of the group. I had to explain that my pessimism was nothing to do with them, but the fact that I felt that there was a good chance that the history of British–Irish relations in the North could easily derail the opportunities that Patten's blueprint had presented.

The main recommendation of that blueprint was the creation of a policing board, an independent public body to be made up of nineteen members, which would be the driver of the new policing service in Northern Ireland and hold it to account for its actions. Noel Gallagher, who had established a close relationship with Brian Cowen, the Irish minister of foreign affairs, was briefing the minister that I was the person from the nationalist community who should be appointed to head up the new board. Within a week or so I got a phone call from then Secretary of State John Reid asking if I would accept an appointment as vice chair of the board, serving under the chairmanship of Desmond Rea. Rea had been a professor in the University of Ulster and before that had worked in the Labour Relations Council. Politically, he would have been considered a moderate unionist.

I had to go in front of a small panel, set up by the NIO, to be interviewed for the position. It was a strange interview. The two interviewers and I all knew that whether I was accepted or rejected for the role would be more the choice of the British and Irish governments than that of the panel members carrying out the interview. All I remember is talking about the need for policing to have a poetic side, understanding the internal influences and sensitivities and not just the externals of the society it policed. It was kind of outlandish, cheeky, and yet relevant. I think it was the only time I ever did an interview for a job, apart from a chat I had with the president of St Columb's College about my application to go forward for the priesthood. Neither would have been considered a proper job interview.

Before the call came from the secretary of state, Gallagher and I had discussed which of the positions, chair or vice chair would be most appropriate and advantageous. If Sinn Féin agreed to take their places on the board, then my presence or position would be of much less importance. But they were having difficulty selling this to their supporters and were not prepared to take their seats on the board. The importance and the necessity of taking their share of responsibility and authority for a new beginning to policing would thus fall on me and I would be entering a lion's den. I would certainly be facing criticism from Sinn Féin, which, in and of itself, I could manage. My fear was that criticism from Sinn Féin would embolden the dissident IRA, who would not have any regard for my well-being.

A lesser, but still annoying, issue was that the old reluctance and even resistance to appointing nationalists to senior positions in law and order was alive and well within Northern politics. The assumption still was that a nationalist could be the vice chair, the second-in-command, but not the chair of such an important and sensitive position. It wasn't the central consideration, but in the tension of entering strange and dangerous terrain, there were few issues that were not sensitive.

A more important part of the debate was around the advantages and the hindrances that both positions threw up. Chair gave greater authority but greater restriction in the enactment of that responsibility. Vice chair carried less status but allowed greater independence and occasional deviancy, which might well be needed on a few occasions. Cowen was consulted and his advice was that vice chair was acceptable. I was very fond of Cowen, but the alacrity with which he accepted our arguments made me slightly suspicious that the Irish government had little expectation that the Policing Board had a great future.

Despite these reservations, I decided that it was the right decision for me to try to play a part in progressing peace by improving one of the most problematical issues for the process. Some may have felt that I had sold out by agreeing to take the 'Queen's shilling', while others who knew me better may have seen my acceptance of this role as consistent with my earlier actions, and probably brave, if possibly a little foolhardy.

My decision was influenced by several discussions I had with former republican prisoners who had all served significant sentences in Long Kesh. They were also all fathers and, perhaps surprisingly, all of them would have supported their children joining the new police service. Their main reason was that they felt their children could make a real difference to the community in such a position, although the starting salary of £19,000 was also a bit of an inducement. I have always found that when people begin to mix idealism with pragmatism like this, then change is possible. However, I had few illusions about the enormity of the cultural, political and structural task that we were facing on the board and was very aware that it could fail as easily as it could succeed.

Like many relationships that work well, Desmond Rea and I began with a blazing row. Literally, before we got our feet under the table, in that we had not yet been allowed to use the offices that were to become our headquarters, we had strong words with each other. Mostly, I must admit, me to him. The UUP had asked him for a meeting (I can't remember if the DUP was also involved) and had insisted that I was not to be invited. Rea had acceded to their request and only informed me about the meeting the following day. That resulted in a fierce argument about how the two positions were going to work and the imperative of working together.

Rea and I are like chalk and cheese. Every weakness I have is one of his strengths and every strength I have is one of his weaknesses. We never had another row that I remember. In fact, we worked well together and grew to trust each other. I admired and appreciated his integrity, his patience, sometimes his stoicism but, above all, his dogged determination to see the job through.

One of the issues on which we initially had a divergence was the relationship of the board with the media. Rea was loath to engage with the press, except in a very formulaic and formal manner. I, on the other hand, saw the media as one of the vehicles that would keep the debate about policing and the proposed Patten reforms high on the agenda. As well as energising efforts at reform, I considered informed debate a more effective security blanket than the paraphernalia that usually accompanies high-profile positions. We both had concerns about safety, but Rea understood that the likelihood of his home or person or family being attacked was much lower than in my case. Apart from the day-to-day work of the board, I saw my role as convincing a broad swathe of people within nationalism and republicanism that policing was making a genuine effort at reflecting their concerns, mostly by attracting their sons and daughters into its ranks, but also by embracing their culture as readily as the other cultures of the North.

The first day in the office, which would have been in November 2001, Rea informed me that he was going to close the bar. In the chairman's office, which he was about to occupy, there was the best-stocked bar I had ever seen in a private establishment. There were not many types of alcohol that were not available. This was a legacy of the Policing Authority that had been in existence during the years of the RUC. Desmond, who came from a strong Methodist background but enjoyed an occasional glass of red wine, asked if I was content for this to happen. I had spent years working with alcohol and drug problems but was tempted to suggest that we keep a few bottles for special occasions or wait until the present stock ran out. However, recognising his determination, I nodded in agreement. This was one of the best decisions made in the first five years. The Policing Board headquarters was to be teetotal and a place of work.

And the work came thick and fast. If the board was to make itself relevant and gain some traction, it was going to need a few early wins. The first came sooner and more emphatically than expected. A new police service wouldn't get far without agreed crests and badges. In most places that would be an incidental, but this was Northern Ireland. The board was constituted in a manner that reflected the political make-up of Northern Ireland, with ten seats reserved for political parties in numbers reflective of their mandate, plus nine independent members, who included the chair and vice chair. We sent a small group of both political and independent members off to a hotel under the chairmanship of Pauline McCabe, one of the independent members and an experienced human relations manager. I don't know what magic Pauline wove, but within days the group came back with unanimous agreement. The PSNI badge would feature the St Patrick's saltire, and six symbols representing different and shared traditions: the scales of justice (representing equality and justice); a crown (a traditional symbol of royalty but not the St Edward's Crown worn by or representing the British sovereign); the harp (a traditional Irish symbol but not the Brian Boru harp used as an official emblem in the Republic); a torch (representing enlightenment and a new beginning); an olive branch (a peace symbol from ancient Greece); and the shamrock.

That agreement should not have been much more than an achievement in good design, but there is nothing simple or straightforward when dealing with change and identity. One of my first jobs was to convince the SDLP that the crown on the badge was acceptable. I was told that there are a variety of crowns but the one to be depicted was not acceptable. At a hastily arranged meeting with a few SDLP representatives and officials from the Irish government, I startled some of them with the extremity of my language when insisting that it was imperative to accept the six symbols.

Alex Attwood was the leader of the SDLP on the board. During the next five years Alex would hear a lot of bad language from me over many issues and we had many heated exchanges, but if I was awarding a prize to the politician who had the greatest influence in making the Policing Board a success, it would go to him. Few had thought that agreement over the crest could be achieved; that unanimous agreement had been arrived at in the subgroup was near miraculous. I don't know if it was my bad language or the elegance of my argument, but Alex came on board, persuaded his colleagues in the party and thankfully the SDLP signed up to the new badge and its symbols. It was a breakthrough that would allow the board to get its teeth into substantive issues.

16

A New Beginning
for Policing

WE MAY HAVE ACHIEVED A small breathing space with the badge, but the next few events, in their gravity and proximity, could easily have choked and suffocated the new Policing Board. The bombing on 15 August 1998 in the town of Omagh in County Tyrone had killed twenty-nine people and injured about 220 others, making it the deadliest single incident of the Troubles in Northern Ireland. It was carried out by a group calling itself the Real IRA, a splinter group that opposed the Provisional IRA's ceasefire and the Good Friday Agreement, signed earlier that year. Telephone warnings were sent almost forty minutes beforehand, but they did not specify the actual location of the car bomb that had been planted, so police inadvertently moved people towards the bomb. That necessitated a Police Ombudsman's report, which would be submitted to the board for its consideration and conclusions.

Nuala O'Loan was the then ombudsman. Thorough, impartial and fearless, she was a high-profile personality who made the office of ombudsman one of the most important in the transformation of policing. Her one weakness was that she could be overly sensitive to criticism, which the politicians quickly spotted and used for their own purposes. I sat through a few meetings where DUP politicians baited O'Loan. They regarded themselves as the guardians of the RUC and, wrongly and unfairly, regarded her as hostile to that legacy – she found it difficult to ignore or circumvent this bating. Then all hell broke loose when she published her report into the Omagh bombing.

The report was published in August 2001. It speculated that the RUC had intelligence from an informer before the explosion that may have allowed them to prevent the attack and that the police had made mistakes in the investigation of the atrocity. It explored whether the police had responded appropriately to the information they had prior to the bomb. Underlying this question was the old accusation of whether Special Branch had withheld critical information from the investigation team. One of the key criticisms in the report was that there was 'a failure of leadership' by Chief Constable Sir Ronnie Flanagan, which meant, in the view of the ombudsman, that 'the victims, their families, the people of Omagh and officers of the RUC have been let down by defective leadership'.

A few days later Ronnie Flanagan rejected the report and the criticism levelled at himself. In a very emotional press conference, he said that he would publicly 'commit suicide' if the accusations in the report were true. Two of the main institutions of policing and accountability were at each other's throats in the full glare of the media and the public around one of the deadliest attacks that had taken place in all the years of the Troubles. There was no hiding from the seriousness of the situation, and the responsibility for absorbing and smoothing out the impact of the turbulence would be that of the new Policing Board, which was barely out of short trousers.

The media coverage around O'Loan's report and Flanagan's response was massive and steadily moving in our direction. Some of it reported on fears that the row could be used as a political football within the board, with unionist members backing Flanagan and nationalists backing O'Loan:

> Ian Paisley Jr, the son of the Rev. Ian Paisley and a Democratic Unionist member of the board, claimed the chief constable's reply was a 'devastating riposte'. Mr Paisley said: 'Sir Ronnie has gone to the nth degree to facilitate people who are on the backs of the police when they should be on the backs of the terrorists.'
>
> But Alex Attwood, a SDLP member of the board, said serious questions remained about Omagh. 'The chief constable has made an elaborate response, and we now have a confusion of detail and various people's interpretations,' he said.

By this stage we had managed to create some coherency in the board. The group of nine independents was the key to that coherence, stability and progress. They respected the mandate of the politicians, but they had managed to coalesce in their concerns for good governance and for renewed and invigorated policing, and their votes, when necessary, would favour those aspirations rather than any perceived or assumed political bias. It was necessary and helpful in those early days to set down a few markers to the politicians that the independent votes were not to be taken for granted and that their nine votes held the balance of power.

But what was being faced now was Becher's Brook in comparison to any earlier difficulties. Northern Ireland was witnessing a Shakespearean drama between two of the most high-profile people in the North, about one of the most awful tragedies that had ever occurred here, just as the community was beginning to believe that the Troubles might be coming to an end. The only political institution extant and functioning at that period was the Policing Board and the disagreements and the interpretations of what occurred or did not occur, and the appropriate way forward, were matters within the responsibility of what was a very new and untested board.

A subgroup of politicians and independents was selected to draw up a response and a set of recommendations that would map a way out of the turmoil and would refocus on the expectations of the victims of Omagh. It would have to reassure the victims' families that those who carried out the atrocity would be pursued by the police in an efficient and professional manner, while also placing the ombudsman's and the police's relationship back on a less fractious setting. I was given the job of chairing the group.

The discussions lasted the best part of three days. I stayed in Belfast for three nights in a row, something I seldom did. After the second night, Desmond Rea very thoughtfully bought me a new shirt.

Everyone was getting nervous and tetchy. Once, during the discussions, I was asked to go to the chair's office to meet some senior civil servants from the NIO. The government was concerned and anxious to know what was happening. That meeting didn't last very long. They had nothing positive to offer and I remember telling them to butt out; this was the concern and the responsibility of the board, and the NIO would be informed when the board had come to its conclusions and recommendations. The board could break its back on this issue, or it could justify its raison d'être. It could not, at that moment, tolerate outside interference, even from the government.

The subgroup drew up a report, which contained an analysis of the conflicting reports from the ombudsman and chief constable and also a series of recommendations that would guide us out of the mess and provide a structure that would address important policing issues and assure the families of those who had been killed in Omagh as well as the public that a proper and thorough policing investigation would proceed. It was a complex and sensitive piece of work that didn't undermine the chief constable but gave more cognisance to the findings of the ombudsman than he would have been comfortable with. The report was agreed with the board and shared with the main protagonists; it would be given to the families and the media the next morning.

Before I left Belfast, tired but happy with what had been achieved, I talked to O'Loan and we agreed that it was a worthy report that she could and would accept. One of her strengths was her ability to gain the trust of those who used her office. She was good at legal, administrative and investigative work, but she also brought a pastoral touch that was not that common within the criminal-justice structures. She had gained the trust of the Omagh families, and I believed her endorsement of the board's report would reassure those families, which in turn would reassure the public that proper procedures were now in place.

I awoke the next morning to a radio interview with a member of one of the Omagh families. He was being critical of the board and its report, though it was not clear if he had even read it. I wasn't unduly concerned. Flanagan was accepting the report, even if a slight reluctance was detectable in the press release. I thought that O'Loan would be coming out with a statement and probably an interview, which would reassure the families that she was welcoming of the report and its recommendations. Those families had been through enough wringers already. But nine, ten, eleven o'clock came and went, and there was nothing from the ombudsman's office. Five times I rang Sam Pollock, O'Loan's loyal chief of staff, asking, even pleading for a statement.

It transpired that the front page of that morning's *News Letter* had a statement from Sammy Wilson criticising O'Loan and her office. Wilson was a DUP politician, a member of the board and a frequent critic of the ombudsman. He had not been on the subcommittee, but his party had been given an early viewing of the report and had endorsed it. My guess was that Wilson had laid a trap and O'Loan had fallen into it. If she refused to endorse the report, it was more than likely that the Omagh families would follow her example, and the arguments would have continued, and all three policing institutions would have been further damaged. However, by lunchtime an endorsement of the report by O'Loan had gone public. Some of us breathed a sigh of relief.

The agreed report and recommendations from the board were a major achievement. Had the board not been able to gather up and reconfigure the fallout from the very public disagreement between the chief constable and the ombudsman about the horrifying bombing of Omagh, what resulted would surely have damaged all three bodies, perhaps beyond repair. Being able to achieve some coherency among its own diverse membership and directing the other two institutions into a less contentious space, displayed the rationale for such a board and provided it with greater confidence in its purpose and ability.

The board's main purpose in statute was to hold the chief constable of the PSNI to account. In other words, authority arose from its power to appoint and sack the chief constable. From this flowed all its other authority to set the standards and create the culture of policing. When the board came into being, Ronnie Flanagan had been in the position of chief constable since 1996. He had joined the RUC the same year I came back from Rome, in 1970. I had never met him prior to joining the board, but he had a very high profile and I had often seen or heard him on television and other media outlets. He had a reputation for being clever, competent, articulate and smooth. Some judged him too smooth.

I had learned on my trip to San Diego with the change management team from the RUC that Flanagan was seen as supportive of the Patten reforms and that his imprimatur and blessing would be vital in enticing the membership of the RUC into support for the PSNI. I was also aware that he had, at one time, been head of Special Branch, a section of the RUC which Patten had described as a 'force within a force'. Special Branch was certainly the aspect of the police that the nationalist community distrusted most.

I was only beginning to get to know Flanagan when the row broke out between himself and the ombudsman. He had always been courteous and supportive of the new board, and certainly showed no signs of opposition or blockage to a new beginning for policing. It wasn't difficult to see how accustomed he had become to getting his own way and how confident he was of his own judgement and, most of all, of his ability to persuade others to his point of view. Everyone who saw it had been shocked at his remarks in the press conference in response to the ombudsman's report. Even before the Policing Board's subcommittee had been convened, Flanagan insisted that Desmond Rea and I sit through a presentation explaining the police response to the Omagh bomb. It was a painful session, an intricate analysis of a complex police investigation with little recognition that this was no longer the problem. The issue may have initially been about forensics and other matters exclusively related to policing, but it had moved past that to become one of credibility and trust. And Flanagan wasn't doing well in maintaining the trust. He was beginning to realise that and was showing signs of uncertainty and fragility.

I especially remember an early morning breakfast with him. He had asked to see Rea and me before a board meeting. Even though I was staying in Belfast overnight, I initially declined to go, telling Rea that he could attend by himself because I was sceptical of the purpose of the meeting, which was to take place at Desmond Rea's home. However, I woke early, changed my mind and walked from my hotel to the house. I kept ringing the bell until I woke Desmond's wife, Maeve, only to learn that the meeting venue had changed to police headquarters.

Arriving late, I was told by Flanagan that he wished to address the board and rehearse the material that he had presented to Rea and me. He was sure that, given this platform, he could convince the board members that he should stay in his post for the foreseeable future and lead the transformation of policing. I remember telling him, repeatedly, that he shouldn't do it because he had lost the confidence of the board and that it would end up in a humiliation, which would be bad for himself and for the board. Under the Patten system, that we were in the throes of implementing, a chief constable, once appointed, had operational independence, but they served at the behest and consent of the board. If any of the members of the board proposed a motion of no confidence in Flanagan, it could result in a very divided vote, damaging the board and making it impossible for the chief constable to continue in his role.

When he came to the board a few hours later, Flanagan didn't do the long presentation but nor did he change many minds. It was clear that he was on his way out and that the system should and would find him a dignified route. It did, initially with a job with Her Majesty's Inspectorate of Constabulary, leading him eventually to the leadership of that organisation. It was clear that the British government believed that they owed Ronnie Flanagan a lot for accepting the political need to move the RUC into the PSNI and for acting as consultant to its birth and its initial stumbling steps.

There was no danger that the mad tempo and drama around policing would abate. On St Patrick's Day 2002, the Special Branch compound in Castlereagh police station was broken into and sensitive information stolen. Who did it and what was stolen? Sinn Féin was quick to deny any republican involvement, but the commentary was soon pointing the finger at the IRA as the only group who had the competence and audacity to strike at the heart of Special Branch. The houses of a few prominent Sinn Féin members, former IRA men's houses, were searched by the police in Derry and Belfast.

No matter who was responsible, the police and the board were back in the spotlight. A couple of days later, Secretary of State John Reid announced that he was appointing Sir John Chilcot to conduct a review into the issues arising from the break-in. Chilcot had been head of the NIO for several years and was there when the peace process was in its infancy. I was interviewed about the appointment on the morning of 22 March 2002 on BBC Radio's *Good Morning Ulster* in my role as vice chair of the Policing Board. I started the interview by praising Chilcot for the very positive role he had played in the peace process before going on to say that there was no need for him to be carrying out the job that John Reid had appointed him to do. I stated that, in my opinion, Chilcot should not be seen as wholly independent, given his previous involvement in Northern Ireland. I suggested that he had been at least partially responsible for MI5 at a time when the peace process was trying to kick off and asserted:

> [This appointment is] going to give a field day to two groups of people: those who complain that the Independent Commission [Patten] is a total disaster and those who complain that its recommendations aren't exactly implemented. In other words, those who say that Patten has brought about all our problems on the one hand and those, like Sinn Féin, who say that its recommendations haven't been implemented. Now the truth of the matter is that we are on a journey which is hopefully, and I think we have made great strides on this, into a new policing arena in which there is going to be policing for all of the community. A police service that is not militarised, a police that has moved out of a war situation into civilian and civilianised policing that is made accountable, open and transparent to the public. That is what we are about, and I think we have made great strides.

I also made it very clear in that interview that the Policing Board had not been consulted about the appointment of Chilcot and that we had made our views on this known to John Reid. The reason I remember this interview so clearly is that it was taped in the Radio Foyle studio in Derry and once it was done, I was leaving the studio to go directly to Belfast for a meeting with Chilcot.

I was only too aware how big a deal the break-in at Castlereagh and the stealing of classified information from the 'Fort Knox' of Special Branch was. I knew that the British government was unlikely to keep its nose out of such a high-profile event and would want to know what was going on with Special Branch and what the Provos were up to, and that the government trusted only its own people. Chilcot was very much one of their people, even if I regarded him as one of the best of them. He began the meeting that morning by thanking me for my kind words, and it ended after an hour or so with me thinking that Chilcot was very likeable and so sharp that he could cut you and you wouldn't even be aware of it until you saw the blood.

I knew that the government was not going to leave the break-in and its consequences to the embryonic Policing Board, but it could easily have been more discreet, announcing that Chilcot's report would not be published. The board had to assert that, at least theoretically, it would be the lead organisation in the investigation, one in which it was becoming clearer that the IRA was behind the break-in. But, as was predictable, the government and Chilcot kept their own council and the board had little involvement in the investigation. Two years later the Northern Bank in Belfast was robbed of £26.5 million in cash. I remember standing at the back of the room in the Policing Board as the recently appointed Chief Constable of the PSNI, Hugh Orde, addressed a packed press conference and said very clearly that he and the PSNI were convinced that the IRA had carried out the bank robbery.

I had once predicted that Sinn Féin would take their seats on the Policing Board a few years after its establishment. That had just gone out the window. There was little or no chance that Sinn Féin was joining a board that was accusing the IRA of breaking into the headquarters of Special Branch, stealing sensitive information and then carrying out one of the biggest bank robberies in the history of Northern Ireland. The timetable for republicans taking their place and their responsibility for law and order within the North of Ireland had just been elongated. That, in turn, meant that my profile was not going to reduce any time soon and it also meant that Hugh Orde, in his new role as chief constable, had better be good, for my sake as well as for the sake of the peace process.

The appointment of a new chief constable had been as daunting for the appointment board as it was for the applicants. Not that there were that many applicants, at least not ones who were likely to be appointed. The chair, vice chair and a mixture of independent and political members had to go through a training regime which, for fear of litigation and judicial review, would drain all humanity out of the process and replace it with a form of robotic interaction. Some of the politicians who had experience in public appointments informed me that they had stopped scribbling any notes or reminders to themselves at these interviews because all such scribblings were gathered up after the interview to be made available in any potential law case; something that was becoming more common. And there was every chance that if someone was unhappy with the way that this high-profile appointment went, it could end up in court.

On the day of the interview, we were treated to the insights of a psychologist, who had put each candidate through a psychometric test and who gave the appointment panel his assessment of the results. He had been provided through the Home Office in London. I was sceptical of the process but greatly impressed by his analysis. I only knew two of the candidates, two local officers, and my contact with them had been limited, but I was surprised at what I considered the accuracy of the insight and assessment of these two officers. In addition to the psychometric evaluation, each candidate gave a presentation before a question-and-answer session. There was great media and public interest in the appointment and diverse opinions on whether the chosen candidate should be someone internal or external. An internal candidate came with the knowledge of the organisation, whereas an external one had the advantage of bringing no baggage to the position. Both arguments had validity, but if all the rigour and strictness of our pre-interview training stood for anything, the appointment was not to be prejudged and was to be based solely on the interview on the day.

But we are talking Northern Ireland here. I can't think of many things in life here even today that exist in a political vacuum or, at least, don't have some political implications, and then we were still in a time where everything, every thought and gesture, was political. There were two internal candidates and one external for the job. The external was Hugh Orde, who had been with the Metropolitan Police in London for most of his career, save a few years when he had worked in Northern Ireland for one of the Stevens inquiries into collusion. Of the internal candidates,

Chris Albison was Special Branch and was probably placed at a disadvantage by the description in the Patten Report of that section of policing being a 'force within a force'. He would surely have had to address that issue somewhere within the interview or presentation. The other, and the one with whom I would have had the most contact, was Alan McQuillan, a long-time assistant chief constable within the RUC. I liked him a lot and I always found him affable, even gregarious, and certainly open and intelligent. While I was writing this book, McQuillan was back in the news for two reasons. First, he had revealed that he was suffering from a rare form of prostate cancer, and second, in a recent documentary on policing, he revealed that after Hugh Orde was appointed, he was encouraged by a DUP politician to take a judicial review against the appointment and if he wasn't prepared to risk the £30,000 or so that it would take to do so, it would be provided. Sammy Wilson quickly responded to this revelation, stating that he had been on the appointment panel and that McQuillan was talking nonsense. He also asked why, if that was the case, it took McQuillan twenty years to come forward.

McQuillan did not do a good interview for the job of chief constable. He knew that himself. He was nervous and not as precise and insightful as I had seen him on other occasions. I don't remember very much about Albison's interview, but I do remember that Orde did a very good interview. He was easily the best of the three candidates. His presentation was the most precise and pertinent, and his answering of questions was competent and insightful.

Rea, during a break in proceedings, consulted me as to whether we could appoint Orde because both Unionist parties were strongly opposed to him. They must have approached Rea to say that they would not endorse Orde's appointment and that their views, as representative of unionism, should be noted and considered. I read somewhere that they thought he was too young for the job. I told Rea that Orde was likely to get the highest vote and, if he did, we were going to appoint him, unionist objection notwithstanding. When he was duly appointed, neither of the two Unionist parties turned up at the press conference where the result was announced. McQuillan didn't go for a judicial review which, as he said himself, he would have lost.

Hugh Orde was an excellent appointment. He had energy, sense and insight. He knew what good policing looked like and had the enthusiasm and the work ethic to imbue most of his staff with the sense that the new police service could work. He faced some opposition from within, but he had the ability to manage even hostile opposition without allowing it to become a distraction. He also had an impressive understanding of the politics of the North. He always made himself available to the political parties and gave them their due respect, but ultimately, he did what he and his command team thought best. He was a real challenge to Sinn Féin because he positively incarnated the thrust of the changes and reforms of the Patten Report. He was a convinced supporter of the Policing Board and its oversight role, and of real and sustained engagement with the broadest community possible.

On a personal level, he and I got on well. We could talk and be honest with each other. He had a good understanding of what I had to do, which was well captured when a few bomb scares were directed at my home. The board was launched in 2001 and I stayed on it for the best part of six years. From the very first months of taking the appointment, the threats towards me began. Bullets in the post, threatening graffiti with my name attached on walls near my home and in other parts of the city. In Dungiven, on the main Belfast Road, a poster condemning the PSNI and me. I passed it every morning I travelled to Belfast. And all of this came before a few bomb hoaxes and a protest outside my home. The most physical attack was the night I was hit over the head with a baseball bat in a pub in Derry. That landed me in hospital for a couple of nights.

From the early months, Jane Kennedy, who was a British minister in the NIO, was very concerned for my security and asked Orde to increase my protection by attaching a policeman to me personally or providing a static police presence outside my house or both. Orde came to tell me of her concern, so I asked what he had told her. He said that he told her I was likely to tell him to f– off. So, I said to him, 'F– off!' A police post outside my house or a plain-clothes policeman walking a few paces behind me would have put a circular target on my back. The dissident IRA, those paramilitaries who did not agree with the Good Friday Agreement and had broken away from the Provisionals, were particularly antagonistic to the PSNI and the new policing arrangements. Their main targets were the police themselves, but people like me who sat on the Policing Board or the local policing committees were also targets. My judgement was that my greatest security was to have no security and to continue to behave in public as per usual. I continued to do that for the six years, and I think it was the right thing to do. But there was one exception. Martin McGuinness advised that the front door of my home was far too exposed, and, on that advice, the NIO put up a higher fence, some lighting and reinforced glass windows.

If the new Chief Constable's appointment was high-profile and controversial, there was another appointment in 2002 that received little attention at the time but, in hindsight, was an important one in the establishment and the rooting of the PSNI. Because it was a part-time position, the appointment of a human rights adviser did not require a panel of board members. It was left to the chair and vice chair. There were four applicants, and I was certain that the third person interviewed, a very impressive woman, was going to get the job. That was until the fourth applicant, a barrister from London, came into the room and within a short period convinced both Rea and me that he was the man for the job. A few years later, he went on to become the head of the criminal justice system in England, then left that position to enter politics, and in 2020 became the leader of the Labour Party in England – in my opinion, he is likely to become the British prime minister someday.

Keir Starmer was very impressive in the short interview that we conducted, and he was equally impressive in the various reports and investigations that he had to do for the board. It was easy to see there was a good intellect at work, coupled with insight and judgement, and he didn't have to be steered through the complex and sensitive political minefield that we were dealing with. The general response to him from the staff and members of the board was that if this man had as much charisma as he had intelligence and integrity, he would go far. But the important thing from the board's perspective, and something that was very important to me, was that he and Hugh Orde got on well and trusted each other.

This was particularly important in relation to the reform of Special Branch. There was a strong conviction within the nationalist community that this 'force within a force' needed to be reined in, reformed and made accountable. The Policing Board, a group made up of people with different backgrounds and political perspectives, was never going to get to grips with such a powerful system and culture, which had been in place for a long time during a dirty and murderous conflict. One possibility was to ask Her Majesty's Inspectorate of Constabulary, an oversight body, which laid down and inspected the implementation of standards in policing throughout the UK, to direct the necessary changes. We called them in on a few occasions. Mostly I found them very thorough and committed to doing a good job, but they were time-limited in their engagement and therefore restricted in their ability to confront such an entrenched institution. So, Orde spent a significant amount of his time restructuring and reforming Special Branch, and he also gave Starmer enormous access and encouragement to get to the heart of the procedures that had become embedded and to recommend ones more suited to an organisation that was not responding to a community in conflict. It was a comfort that someone employed and responsible to the board was overseeing and accessing that piece of important work.

Apart from the travelling up and down to Belfast and elsewhere, I enjoyed those years. I knew that I had an aptitude for understanding the dynamics of organisations and the change mechanisms, as they are called nowadays, that are often needed to keep matters healthy. My closest allies on the board, both members and staff, often joked that I was good on the big stuff and not so good on the wee stuff. There was truth in that, but I rejected the implications of the criticism in favour of my own judgement that, in the first few years of the board's existence, the big political and institutional issues would make or break the board and that the smaller issues would come into their own after the board had laid down some strong roots.

Some people said that I was simply keeping the seat warm for Sinn Féin. I understood that argument, but it was much too simplistic and didn't fully explain the breadth and the depth of the issue. Sinn Féin was always going to join the board – the only question was when. Politics has its own logic and when the decommissioning of arms happened, the inevitable consequence was that every political party had to take its share of responsibility and oversight for the policing of society. I was annoyed and disappointed that Sinn Féin was so slow in coming to that conclusion, and even more disappointed that it didn't take its seats on the board while I was there. However, I had attended some of the meetings that the party had held amongst its own supporters and the depth of anger of some of them was visceral. In the end, though, political logic would have its way.

I was more aware of warming the seat for that large group of nationalists who were inherently law-abiding and respectful of law and order and a stable society. They were nationalists who sometimes voted Sinn Féin and, before that, the SDLP when John Hume was in charge. They were likely to be involved with the GAA and/or the Catholic Church. They had been antagonised by and antagonistic to the RUC for so long that any move across the bridge to policing would be hesitant, cautious and fearful.

On the morning of the publication of his report, Chris Patten had made a direct and forthright appeal to the leaders of nationalism and Catholicism. He called upon priests, teachers and politicians to encourage young Catholics and young nationalists to join the new police service. In my six years on the board, a steady number of the sons and daughters of that demographic did join the PSNI. They didn't all come from the six Northern Irish counties of Ulster – a surprising number came from the other three counties of the province with a few stragglers from further down the country. The feedback we got from them was generally positive in the reception they received from fellow recruits from a unionist background and from the police themselves.

When Sinn Féin eventually took its seats on the board, it did so with a strong attitude of holding the police to account and a weakish expression of support. That hesitancy left the Catholic community uncertain of how to react and how to interact with the new police service. Sinn Féin's hesitancy and caution was mostly to placate the hardliners, but it made it very difficult to enable a new beginning to policing. Instead of embracing and promoting the PSNI as being a child of the peace process and encouraging young nationalists to join and own it, the party opted for the 'prove to us that you have changed' school of politics. This was despite having watched unionism adopt the same 'prove to us' policy towards Sinn Féin on innumerable occasions and having seen the ineptitude of that type of political strategy.

That hesitancy and caution had further consequences. It allowed the various strands of dissident republicans – the Real IRA, the Continuity IRA and others – to be bolder in their opposition to the new police service. Bold enough to kill or maim a few new recruits, bold enough to plant bombs at the homes and under the vehicles of members of the District Policing Partnerships and the civilian members of the police liaison committees established in every council district. Bold enough to attack my home on a few occasions and bold enough to hit me over the head with a baseball bat in a pub one evening when watching a football match with my youngest son. Sinn Féin condemned all those actions and challenged the dissident republicans to desist from such violence, but the fact that the party was in contention with the new policing structures made it easier for the dissidents.

I would contend that political parties have the right, even the duty, to contest that which they disagree with, but by the time Sinn Féin took its seats on the Policing Board, not one single item of the party's legislation or procedure had been changed from the time that I had started as vice chair of the board. The delay in joining the board turned out to be a matter of internal party management rather than a principled objection.

The attack in the pub was not the first time my life was threatened. A report in the *Derry News* in July 2003 noted:

> Dissident republicans claimed last night that a hoax bomb attack at the Derry home of the Policing Board deputy Chairman should serve as a warning to all District Policing Partnerships (DPP) members that they could be targeted.
>
> Sources close to the Real IRA told the *Derry News* that the van carrying the hoax device was left close to Denis Bradley's home on Monday night to demonstrate that they were prepared to carry out attacks against both Policing Board and DPP members.
>
> The source linked the hoax to recent police house raids on dissident republicans in Derry and Belfast. He warned that if such 'harassment' continued, the next time the bomb will be real. The Bradley family and some neighbours were evacuated from their homes before the 'attack' was finally declared a hoax.

Many politicians and public figures have stated that attacks on their family are more painful than attacks on themselves. I agree with that. On one occasion, petrol bombs were thrown at my house, setting the front door alight. I was in Belfast, and Mary and my son Eoin were at home. Another time, my daughter, Laura, was at home alone when a protest group approached and tried to enter the house before she had an opportunity to lock the door. Those are the events that hurt people the most, and the people who are mostly hurt, because of the male-dominated nature of our society, are women and children. There is something unmanly and cowardly about such actions.

The attack on myself was in a pub. Seeking somewhere that was showing a Derry City football match, my younger son and I arrived in a pub in the parish where I had once been a priest. It could not have been a planned attack, but I was made aware that a few dissident republicans had arrived. I was told later that one of them was seen to leave the pub and it was sometime after that that a young man came in and hit me over the head with a baseball bat. I have vague memories of the kerfuffle in the bar, a doctor holding a towel to my head, being put into an ambulance, talking to Eamon Deane, with whom I had set up the Bogside Community Association, on the way to the hospital, talking to and consoling the very nervous young junior doctor who was about to stitch up my wounds, Mary arriving and holding my hand during all of it as I talked constantly, and Mark Durkan and Martin McGuinness turning up in the treatment room. During all of this I was strongly conscious that I didn't want to fall into unconsciousness. Staying in control was a strong urge.

After two nights in hospital, I was allowed home. There was a lot of media interest, but I was insistent that I would not go out the main door. I didn't want anyone taking photographs of me in that condition, with a bandaged-up mouth, nose and forehead.

I would have found those photographs too great an intrusion. A few days later, McGuinness called at my house to see how I was doing. As he was leaving, he said, 'You know, of course, it is not you they are really after, it is me.' No truer words were ever spoken. I was only a pale substitute for the real obstacle to dissident republicanism. McGuinness was the real blockage, the wall that had to be climbed or removed if this breakaway brand of republicanism was to be any more than a stone in the shoe to the evolving politics. McGuinness was the one who would eventually stand beside Chief Constable Hugh Orde and describe the dissidents as traitors to Ireland and militarily pathetic. Thankfully, they never did take McGuinness out and they never became any more than a stone in that shoe.

17

Legacy

I REMARKED IN MI5 HEADQUARTERS in London that I had concluded that the past, the legacy of forty years of conflict, was like a volcano that would one day explode. The chief of MI5 in Northern Ireland, who was at that meeting with his boss, along with Robin Eames and me, said that he didn't see it as a volcano but rather as a tsunami that would keep flooding the political terrain of Northern Ireland. My description was wrong; his continues to be accurate. This was one of hundreds of meetings, gathering the views of thousands of victims of the Troubles and the insights of the multitude of organisations who were engaged in or affected by the Troubles.

The conversation about the legacy of the past and how to deal with it had started for me on a cold November morning in Derry, the bitter wind scourging my face as I made my way from the car to the City Hotel. I was never a lover of early morning meetings, always in need of a few cups of warm tea before my mind gets in motion. I never took much notice of people's official titles, but by this stage I knew that Robert Hannigan was one of the most influential officials in the NIO. We were not bosom pals, but we were at ease with each other. He had a direct line to Downing Street and that was confirmed by his CV after he left the North, when he became intelligence adviser to the prime minister and then director of government communications headquarters, or GCHQ as it is better known. When I was meeting with him, his reputation was that he was Jonathan Powell's man, and Powell was Tony Blair's man in the North. The meeting was to suss out if I would jointly head up a group to consult and recommend on how to deal with the legacy of the past.

In the weeks before I left the Policing Board, I had pleaded with Hannigan not to damage the incoming board by removing too many of the then independent members. In the government's anxiety to get the Stormont Executive re-established, it was handing out goodies to the political parties and I had heard that the DUP (Sammy Wilson or Ian Paisley or both) had been insisting that some of the board's independents should not be re-appointed. It was a bit of revenge for some lost board battles. My plea to Hannigan was that this was not a red line, a deal-breaker for the DUP, but that it would weaken the board, which would be a bad result. I was aware of the contradiction in arguing that certain people be retained on the board while I was walking away. My justification was that there was still work to be done and the board needed to stay strong, at least for a time yet.

For my own part, I believed that appointments to public bodies should be broad in their embrace and, in most circumstances, short in their duration. On top of that, I owed it to my family to spend more time at home. While I loved living in Derry, one of the disadvantages of its location is having to travel everywhere. It can be a day's work just to get to your work. I also thought that my main contribution was already mostly made. Sinn Féin was readying itself to join the board and their presence would complete the complement of political representation. Polling figures were showing that public confidence in the police was high and the work that remained was more bureaucratic than political.

My initial response to Robert Hannigan, on that cold November morning, was to ask him if he was out of his tiny mind. Some weeks previously I had accidently heard a programme on BBC Radio 4 documenting the history and legacy of the Spanish Civil War and how, after forty and more years, it was still toxic in Spanish politics. After some serious hesitation, my response to the request from the British government to take part in a consultation to address the legacy of the past was firstly to learn the mind of the Irish government. I needed to know its views. I told Hannigan that I would come back to him when I had scouted the terrain.

The setting and timing for the meeting with the Irish was better than the one with Robert Hannigan – a pleasant restaurant of an evening in Derry. This was the era when the British and Irish governments were mostly working hand in hand. Apart from co-operation on the day-to-day political front, there was broad agreement on decommissioning, policing and paramilitary disbandment. In fact, some people, including me, had become annoyed by what appeared to be a graduated lessening of engagement by the Irish government in the affairs of the North. I was never sure whether it was a consequence of the financial storm that was stirring in Ireland and indeed in the rest of the world, or because it was the instinct of their Department of Foreign Affairs to revert to a more cautious and conservative approach once the immediate crisis had receded and the politicians had turned their attention elsewhere.

Pat Hennessy, the then director general of Anglo-Irish affairs, hosted the dinner. He was very clear about the Irish government's stance. There had already been a joint British–Irish approach when Judge Peter Cory, a Canadian, was asked to examine files relating to some legacy deaths. The judge's findings that there should be four public inquiries – three under the auspices of the British and one under the Irish – had been agreed and the Irish government saw no need for its further involvement in legacy issues. It was not in disagreement that a fully comprehensive process should take place but felt that it was the responsibility of the British government – the Irish would not be jointly engaging with it.

I was basically being told by Hennessy that the Irish government had defined the limits of its responsibility for the Troubles and the limits of its responsibility in responding to the consequences. I debated with him about this approach. I mentioned the radio programme documenting the Spanish Civil War and how the embers of that conflict were continuing to flare up decades later. I revealed my own doubts and reservations as to how and if the legacy could be addressed and said that while I agreed the British had the primary responsibility, it was a fact that the best outcomes and sustainability were achieved when both governments worked together. I argued that the Irish government had a vital responsibility and role in trying to heal some of the ongoing wounds. I pointed out that his title was 'Anglo-Irish', that the legacy was the outworking of those affairs and that the new policing structures were going to be burdened by that legacy, in that the police were still responsible for investigations and prosecutions. Those and other arguments were on the menu that night.

The only dent I made was that the Irish government would appoint an observer to whatever process was established, but they would not formally be part of the commissioning process. Retrospective musings are dangerous, in that they cannot capture the full spectrum of possibility, including the accidental and the bizarre. Acknowledging those limitations, I have often thought that the effort to deal with the legacy of the past was badly damaged by the Irish government's decision to stand aside and take the role of an observer.

The Department of Foreign Affairs would have told you then, and would tell you even more decisively today, that the Good Friday Agreement only worked when the two governments were singing from the same hymn sheet. Had either of these governments stood alone on the Good Friday Agreement, or on the decommissioning of arms and most especially on the new policing proposals, then it is doubtful if we would have made much progress. However, when the report on the past compiled by our group, officially called the Consultative Group on the Past, was published (Eames/Bradley became the shorthand title for the report) and the inevitable outcry arose, there was only one government who had the responsibility to absorb and push beyond the sectional responses of political parties and victims. Had the Irish government been a co-sponsor and thus a co-owner of the report, had they been at the heart of the discussions and the decisions (or more accurately the non-decisions) that followed, there is a greater possibility that the recommendations of the report would have been implemented. To me it is ironic that currently the Irish government is critical of British proposals to deal with the legacy and this is one of the issues creating deep divisions between the two governments.

The same analysis and criticism that I direct at the Irish government must also be directed at myself. I preach that the

Anglo-Irish agreements are the foundational stones of peace and change in Northern Ireland and it is those agreements that are sustainable and transformational. I have argued that the Good Friday Agreement is an incarnation of these Anglo-Irish decisions. I could also accuse myself of being so obsessed with the need for the IRA and the British to engage to bring about an end to violence that I initially underplayed the importance of the Irish government. An argument could be made that the backchannel of Duddy, Gallager and myself should have concurrently created another backchannel to the Irish government, and that might have facilitated an end to violence at an earlier stage. That is partly the reason I give so much credit to Noel Gallagher in his efforts to draw in and keep the Irish government fully engaged. However, it is also true that Gallagher had little belief that the legacy of the past could in any way be successfully addressed outside of the natural process of the deaths of the combatants and victims, so he wasn't any great help in convincing the Irish government that dealing with that legacy should be a joint project.

Whatever about all those maybes, the pertinent question here is why I agreed to co-chair the Consultative Group on the Past. Why did I not follow my own insight and say no? I can lay out the excuse that they would have just asked someone else who might have had less experience than me. Or that I had become convinced that the past was a swamp that was so difficult to traverse that it would clog and perhaps even suffocate the peace and the political progress that had been achieved. I did think all those things, but I also believe that my ego played a large part in my acceptance of the position of co-chair along with Robin Eames, the former Church of Ireland archbishop. I think I convinced myself that this was my final contribution to the work for peace that I had accidentally stumbled into as a young curate way back in the Long Tower. I have already referred to a sermon I gave about St Paul's ego and the thorn that plagued him all his life. I know that thorn very well.

I had another meeting with Robert Hannigan and the Northern Ireland Secretary of State, Peter Hain, and said that I would do the job if they let me have a say in who would make up the membership of the Consultative Group and the civil servants who would service the group. They agreed.

Whatever my doubts and my ego, they didn't prevent the ultimate report from being a very good piece of work. In fact, it was more than that. It was an excellent piece of work. When the final conclusions of an examination and a response to such a fraught and complex issue are exposed to the light, there is the worry that the underlying premise gets it wrong or that some essential element has been overlooked or ignored. However, in the thirteen years since that report was published, nothing has exposed its narrative or its recommendations as being misplaced or wrong. That is down to the people who made up the group, mostly Church people interspersed with two from the sporting world. We undertook the most extensive consultation ever undertaken in this part of the world. The group knew how to listen and how to interpret the underlying issues and we were enabled by a small number of very capable civil servants, who sensitively dealt with the victims of the Troubles, with suspicious politicians and with legal conundrums.

Thirteen years later and the past is still a swamp that has become even more cloying due to the continuing disagreements. Initially these were between the local political parties, sometimes supported and at other times provoked by sections of the victim and survivor community. An agreement on how to deal with the past, among other things, called the 'Stormont House Agreement', was announced in 2014. The Irish government, having refused to co-sponsor the work of the Consultative Group and having been officially absent when the group published its recommendations, changed its position and was part of these negotiations. The agreement was between the two governments and local politicians, and it was broadly based on the recommendations of our Consultative Group. It was never implemented and eventually fell apart. Presently all the Northern political parties and the Irish government are united in their opposition to a legacy bill drawn up by the British and voted into law in Westminster, mostly aimed at accommodating British Army veterans. It is about to be challenged in court by victims' groups, while the Irish government is taking a legal challenge at a European level.

In the days and weeks following the publication of the consultative report, the mother of all rows broke out. It was probably a release of all the pent-up hurt and anger from the previous forty years and a reflection of all the pain inflicted during that time. The main target of the anger was the recommendation that the nearest relative of anyone who died because of the conflict in Northern Ireland from January 1966 should receive a one-off, ex-gratia recognition payment of £12,000. The problem arose in defining who was a victim, and because we could find no consensus for that in the consultation, we proposed using the one in Article 3, Paragraph 1 of the Victims and Survivors (Northern Ireland) Order 2006, where a victim and survivor is defined as 'someone who is or has been physically or psychologically injured as a result of or in consequence of a conflict-related incident; someone who provides a substantial amount of care on a regular basis for an individual; someone who has been bereaved as a result or in consequence of a conflict-related incident'. It was the only formal definition that had been determined and passed by the Westminster parliament and the only one that included a bereaved person. Of course, it is very broad and inclusive, which meant that for our purposes it would include families of IRA and loyalist paramilitaries as well as those of civilians and British soldiers.

Peter Robinson, the First Minister in the Stormont Executive of that time, and all his colleagues would not have had time to read the report before proclaiming that under no circumstances would they accept any equivalence between paramilitaries and the forces of law and order. The response from the loudest voices on the unionist side centred on the equivalence issue, while on the nationalist side they focused on the hierarchy of victims that lack of equivalence would create. That division of views between nationalists and unionists was eminently predictable. It was the reason the report stated that the two national governments had to take responsibility for implementing the report, giving the local Executive only a consultative role. The media commentary to this day is that the £12,000 recommendation killed off the report. I find that commentary annoying and saddening. It is an inditement of the poor quality of much of the analysis done by some of the local media.

On the night before the launch of the report, there was a discussion amongst group members about which and how many of the recommendations would create an explosive reaction. The £12,000 was not at the top of the list because unionist politicians had been part of the discussion of the statutory definition of a victim passed at Westminster, so it would be embarrassing for them to oppose this now, and nationalist politicians should have no problems with it. The recommendation that I thought would create a strong reaction was one around expunging prisoners' records. But, in truth, we were not unduly worried which recommendations would evoke these reactions. Governments expect such reactions about sensitive issues and have their methods of using the hostility to their advantage – that is if they want to implement the core. We expected that they would reject or long-finger one or more of the most contested recommendations, allowing objectors to have their input, while pushing ahead with the substantive aspects.

The Consultative Group had been appointed by Secretary of State Peter Hain, but the legwork had been done by Robert Hannigan and he had been promoted into 10 Downing Street shortly after we began working. I tried to keep in contact with Hannigan to have a steer for the group on any changing political winds. But I was pushed off, diplomatically of course. I rang him one day to be told that he was painting a room in a new house and that he would get back to me. I might still be waiting on that call had we not bumped into each other two years later outside Westminster Cathedral after an Ash Wednesday Mass, me with Lenten ashes on my forehead. I wasn't sure if he had ashes or not, and I was too delicate to ask if he had been at the Mass, but I think he had been.

We went for a quick coffee. I had to rush to a meeting with the Northern Ireland Affairs Committee and he was rushing off to somewhere in Whitehall. The quick conversation was mostly taken up with the cost of the proposals contained in the report. He thought the £300 million that we estimated the five years' work would cost was prohibitive. I countered that a £100 million of that would be going to the legacy of depression, trauma and addiction, and that one public inquiry alone had cost more than £200 million. Within the short conversation I think I detected a regret that we had not come up with a proposal for something more akin to an amnesty or, at least, a quicker closing down of legacy cases.

I wasn't completely surprised at his reference to the finance aspect. These were the years following the collapse of Lehman Brothers and the financial collapse that had taken the full attention of governments across the world. When Robin Eames and I met with the British Prime Minister Gordon Brown for an hour during the consultation, we agreed that we were talking to a distracted and near-exhausted politician. Later, when we had a courtesy hour with Taoiseach Brian Cowen, even though the Irish government had never taken ownership of our process, Robin and I agreed that Cowen was at the same stage of near collapse. There could not have been a worse time to present a report that carried the baggage of years of hurt and recrimination, one that was not central to the concerns of the larger constituency of either government.

It is often said that a politician who has not initiated or commissioned a project will be less committed to its implementation. That is also true of senior civil servants. I was beginning to detect a feeling of resentment from the new team of civil servants in the NIO towards Hannigan, which really indicated a resentment towards Jonathan Powell and his team from Downing Street, who had successfully pushed through the Good Friday Agreement. I was picking up disparaging remarks about 'Hanniganisms'. There was tension also between the native Northern Ireland civil servants and those sent over from London to work with the secretary of state. Civil servants can be as petty as their political masters.

The Northern Ireland ones informed me that the London ones wanted the report binned the day it was published.

Robert Eames and I had established a close relationship with the new Secretary of State, Shaun Woodward. Woodward was not always highly regarded by the Northern Ireland political parties, but we found him very committed and genuinely fond of the place and its people. It might be wishful thinking on my part, but I believe that had Woodward had the weight of the Department of Foreign Affairs, personified in Eamon Gilmore or Simon Coveney, standing with him in ownership of the report, the outcome might have been different. The British never rejected the report, they just let it drift, and when the political temperature around legacy overheated, they set up a new process or a new consultation, borrowing the core recommendations of the Eames/Bradley report but allowing the local political parties to bed those in a governance structure that was ill-defined and overpopulated. Our report had suggested governance by three people, the local parties suggested something in the order of thirty. That agreement for a time seemed to have a chance of implementation, until the local parties pulled it apart and the British government bowed to the influence of a section of the Conservative Party who prioritised the demands of soldiers who had served in Northern Ireland during the Troubles years. And so, the legacy of our Troubles remains contentious and comprehensively unaddressed to the present day.

Sometimes I feel angry, but more often sad, at what is happening about legacy. I know that most efforts, in so many countries, at dealing with the past have been unsuccessful. But we had a chance. The Consultative Report was specific, time-limited, comprehensive and workable. It would not have solved everything, but it would have smoothed out an amount of the bitterness and recrimination. It would have delivered to the greatest number of victims and survivors of the Troubles the greatest possible amount of recognition, of compensation, of truth and of justice. It would also have delivered to society a greater insight and understanding of the forty years of violence and mayhem.

One of the main themes of our report was that it was wrong, probably futile, to tackle legacy in a partial or sectional way. If there was to be any chance of success, the past had to be addressed comprehensively. Looking around the world at attempts to address the legacy of so many conflicts, the conclusion has to be that not many of them have been successful or beneficial to their country, not even in South Africa, a country which attracts the greatest attention and praise. We had a chance, but we allowed the greater need to be destroyed by more cautious and introverted views and positions. It is probably a forlorn hope but maybe, when those more sectional interests are exposed as inadequate, some of the spirit and wisdom contained in the Consultative Report will be resurrected and applied.

18

Apologia

ON 25 SEPTEMBER 2005 *The Sunday Times* ran a profile entitled 'Blessed be a peacemaker with hardest head of all', accompanied by an unflattering but recognisable face sketch of me with the caption: 'He loves being centre stage. In another life he would have fulfilled his ambitions by going into politics.' This was published the weekend after I was hit on the head with a baseball bat. After a description of the attack, my two days in hospital, and the strength and diversity of condemnation of the attack, there is a short analysis: 'Many thought that Bradley, despite his sporadic spats with virtually all political groupings, was untouchable. He was the curate who gave the last rites to three dying men on Bloody Sunday; the mentor who helped negotiate the IRA ceasefire; the pioneering campaigner who built shelters for down-and-outs and treatment centres for drug addicts.'

Brendan Duddy is quoted: 'His collar gave him that extra bit of authority back then. The Provos listened very intently to the church. The priest's word was law. But Denis also had a very strong notion of salvation, wanting to save people. Not in a religious sense but in the context of the reality of the moment. He was always watching out for people who needed to be saved.'

The article also says that both sides of the conflict confessed to me. It quoted me as saying that I refused to name members of the IRA at the Bloody Sunday inquiry, citing confessional confidentiality: 'Many people spoke to me about things, people from the Provisional IRA, people from the Official IRA, people from the British Army, people from the RUC. Most of it would have been confidential and I would have considered it confessional.'

But the comment that intrigued me most was anonymous: '"He's a hard man to dislike," comments someone who knows him well. "In one sense, he's your typical parish priest – arrogant, full of self-belief. And this can be irritating, particularly if he is barking up the wrong tree. But he has a real charisma. Irrespective of his policing or political pronouncements, there is always a warmth about him."'

A typical parish priest – arrogant, full of self-belief – is a description you would think I would want to run away from, and I would if it didn't strike me as being close to the bone. The 'priest' part of me is not something I ever did or could run away from. It is part of who I am. At the ceremony when you are ordained a priest, the words 'you are a priest forever according to the order of Melchizedek' are solemnly said. Those words were said over me, and I don't renounce them. However, I would like a discussion on the meaning, the definition of the word 'priest'. For me, the definition would be very different today from the meaning it held for me at the time I was ordained, and the one which sections of the Catholic Church still want to hold on to. I would want to argue the falsehood of that definition, but this is not the place nor the time for that.

The 'parish' bit is something to which I still have a deep attachment. I think I deposited the interest and the study of social justice embodied in the Chavezs, the Dorothy Days, the Berrigans and the Saul Alinskys of this world into an image of what a parish should be. Of course, the concept that is in my head is seldom realistic, but every so often you get a glimpse of the importance of and the need for parish. Despite the narrowness, the male clericalism, the twisted theology and the emotional repression that led to the pathetic and hateful sexual scandals within Catholicism, every so often the importance and the beauty of a faith-led community of people, a parish, is to be seen within the life of Ireland. It would be an awful shame if we were to lose that sense of the local, the hope that arises from a very fragile faith and the love that can flow from both.

This is being written in the days that followed the tragic deaths of ten people in a freak gas explosion in the small village of Creeslough in County Donegal. It is a small village on a peninsula adjacent to the Inishowen peninsula where I was born and grew up. Creeslough always had a place in my heart because our next-door neighbour used to sit at the piano in our front room to play and sing the song, 'Cutting the Corn in Creeslough Today'. The rituals and liturgies needed to embrace and encompass such a tragedy and such a weight of grief are currently being found in that small parish and within the beautiful church that sits at the foot of Muckish Mountain.

Ireland has mercifully changed and mostly separated itself from the dominating and domineering Catholic Church structures, but the people are instinctively appreciative and protective of the cult and the culture that is to be found at the heart of Catholicism and the life of the parish. Occasionally, I am pulled into a conversation about faith and/or the existence of God. It nearly always begins with the sentence: 'You were a priest, so you would know about these things.' I have to admit that I know no more about 'these things' than anyone else.

About ten years ago I wrote a column for *The Irish News* on a Good Friday that captured some of my own beliefs. It is a simple piece, but I cherish it as one of the best columns I ever wrote. It is reproduced here because it gives a flavour of the faith that I still cling to and a small feel of the theological texture that I think the Catholic Church sometimes, at its best, still retains and needs to express more confidently in the future:

The little church sat on the side of a dark mountain. The low flat land, out of which the mountain sprang, fingers of fields, stretched out to touch the sea. The word had gone out around the parish that a simple form of confessions could be had at the wee dark church. You wouldn't have to tell the priest your sins. You would just have to ask for forgiveness, and you would be given absolution. Not much public banter about it – too intimate for that – but nevertheless you could feel the frisson. I arrived at the church early, but the car park was already half full.

Inside was a healthy crowd huddled at the back of the church. There was a smattering of old and young, men and women, married and single. The priest came out and said that we should come forward to the altar in a single line. He said that many people hadn't been to confession for many years and wouldn't remember the words of the ritual. No need to be embarrassed. No need to remember any formula. No need to list your sins. Just come forward and tell the priest that you have sinned, and he would speak the words of forgiveness.

Earlier in the day the same priest and two women from the parish had read the long Gospel. The events of Palm Sunday, the eucharistic meal of Holy Thursday and the violence, torture and death of Good Friday. Maybe it was the hangover of those readings, maybe it was the setting of the little church at the side of the dark mountain or maybe it was because I hadn't been to confession for years, but for whatever one, or all, of those reasons I found the experience moving and memorable. It was easy to feel what it was like to be in Jerusalem all those years ago and to hear Jesus say to you that your sins were forgiven and to go and sin no more. It was easy to ponder the wonder of those words and equally easy to ponder how they would give rise to scandal. That was the reaction when they were first spoken. There were those who found it possible to go with the words and with the man who spoke them. There were those who thought it scandalous that any man takes it upon himself to speak as though he were God.

Those differences project themselves into our times. Between then and now, there are fewer people who would give any credence to the existence of a God, never mind to Christ's claim that he came from God the Father. The debate and the arguments have once again taken a central place in the imagination and the concerns of humankind. The debate has been challenging but too often angry and crude. Richard Dawkins and Christopher Hitchens were the ones who best captured the public imagination, and while they argued with scholarship and conviction for the non-existence of a deity, they were sometimes crude and intemperate. But if they were, they were well matched by the arrogance and superciliousness of the Christian Churches, especially the Catholic Church. As Christ had warned, the Churches had sinned grievously with their obsession and their loyalty to their various temples rather than to the radical and magnificent explanation of human living and dying that is found in the life and death of Jesus and in his teaching as best found in the Sermon on the Mount.

Faith is always a difficult walk between belief and doubt, between hope and despair. It is too delicate to be arrogant, too fragile to be severe. It lives between the aridness of human failings and the wonder of human possibility.

It talks to a God who may not even be there and yet it delights in the possibility of being involved in the continuous creation of the universe. It realised how incongruous it is to stand before a man (hopefully soon before a woman) and to ask that sin be forgiven in the name of Jesus. It knows how radical and transformative that is, and if it is not foolish, how amazingly comforting it is.

It does all this because it sees in Jesus someone who has understood and explained the human heart better than anyone else. It does it because he describes a here and now and an after now that finds an echo in our being.

Leaving the spirituality and the theology aside, the column about the small church was really a long-winded response to the statement in the *Sunday Times* profile that in another life I would have entered politics. I can understand why that appears to be the case, but I don't think it is true. While I have high regard for those who enter politics and an appreciation of its importance in the affairs of the world, and even though I get annoyed with those who deride politics, it doesn't go to the depths of human discourse and relationships that attract me.

Politics became a large part of my life because of the accident of time and place. To respond to what was going on around me, to the violence and the layered political tensions, it was necessary to engage with the world of politics or, perhaps more accurately, to engage with the void that was present because of the lack of politics. I have described the desire to accompany Hume to his meeting on the evening we and others were soaked by water cannon. But that was more akin to being part of a theatrical drama and then being removed from the action while the drama continued. Which brings me back to the quotation in *The Sunday Times* that 'he loves being centre stage'. I can't run away from that because my ego is still healthy and surprisingly active for a man of my age.

If these musings are an examination of motivation, I think it would be honest to say that the confessional box and the group therapy that I practised in the Northlands Treatment Centre for ten or twelve years would be responsible for demoting politics to a second place in my life. The confessional box (it really was just a box in those years) allowed me into the lives of people in a fashion that moved me much deeper than politics ever could and moved me into my own feelings and motivations. But I can't deny that I had an attraction to politics. The TV series *The West Wing* was, for years, my favourite programme. I have gone back to it time and time again. When annoyed or at a loose end, I would often watch a few episodes. I am as big a sucker as the next man for the emotional and sentimental manipulation for which Aaron Sorkin, the writer, has a genius.

I have only been to America four times in my life. Two of those trips were to Washington DC and on one of those occasions I made it to the West Wing. In the first year of the new Policing Board there was an invite to the St Patrick's Day events in the American capital. All the political parties in Ireland, North and South, like to be represented, but I didn't go. Desmond Rea likes to tell the story that about ten people were invited into the Oval Office, including himself, Gerry Adams and Martin McGuinness. McGuinness asked Rea where I was, only to be told that I had said I wouldn't be found dead attending an occasion hosted by the then president, George Bush, and that they shouldn't either. Rea said that McGuinness enjoyed that. The irony is that I went to Washington the following year and attended an event in the White House with about a hundred people. It was addressed by George Bush and I was more impressed by his speech than I wanted to be.

Early in 2022 the BBC asked me to take part in a programme examining the year 1972, probably the worst year for the escalation of violence and its consequences in the the decades that followed. The producer informed me that the BBC had discovered a documentary filmed in that year with surprisingly strong access to footage of IRA training and bomb-making, as well as to funerals and community unrest. It seems it was made by an American company and, peculiarly, had never been broadcast. They told me that there was footage in it of me presiding at a graveside. They thought it was the funeral of Colm Keenan, one of the two young men who was shot dead in Meenan Park, whom I anointed on the night of his death and the following day was visited by a young British officer who thought he might have shot him. When I talk about those years and the memories begin to take hold, I realise how much of the detail, the dates, the exact places, the people present, the chronology, how much of all that I quite often get wrong or confused, but how accurate my emotional memory still is.

The reminiscing, the books and the documentaries are a good sign that the worst of the violence has morphed into antagonisms and rows about identity and the political future of Ireland, North and South. BBC documentaries about the Troubles and books like this one were seldom published while the violence was still in full flow. And while there remains a small group of dissident republicans and loyalists who hold on to the conviction that violence is acceptable and necessary for whatever cause they espouse, the people and the politics have moved to a different place. The North is a place still fraught with tensions and differences, but slowly, very slowly, it is coming to a realisation that a settled and agreed long-term political agreement cannot be avoided for all that much longer.

Some of the people whose lives interwove with my own and who inhabit the pages of this book are now dead. Brendan Duddy had a severe stroke, which was cruel beyond belief. Its severity destroyed two of the physical attributes that were so important to him and indicative of him. Long before the streets of every town and city were packed with marathon runners, Brendan was winning cross-country races. He would tell the story of how, when he was Ulster champion, he accidently came up against an American soldier and athlete who was stationed in Derry and who beat him out of sight in a race. It took him a year, training with the American, to match him. He often told this story as a cautionary tale for Irish politicians, including Sinn Féin, when they were engaging with British politicians in the task of bringing about a united and shared Ireland. The moral of the story was that when you think you are good, it is a good thing to discover that you are not yet good enough.

He also lost his voice. It was not easy to be around him during his final years and feel his frustration at not being able to engage in conversation. When Duddy died, Michael Oatley, the MI6 man, turned up at his funeral, as did Peter Taylor, the documentary maker who had made a film about him – he gave a eulogy. I looked around the church and the funeral lunch to see if the man known to us as Fred – Robert McLarnon, or Colin Ferguson as it appeared on his business card – had come. He hadn't. He turned up on television more recently in a very short film made by Peter Taylor. He said that he was proud of whatever small contribution he had made to the peace process.

John Hume won plaudits and awards galore. What he didn't get was the health to enjoy his retirement. In the period around the Good Friday Agreement, his health deteriorated. The multiple years of stress and the effects of a few medical operations resulted in the deterioration of his memory. It was particularly hard on his wife, Pat, who had carried and absorbed a great part of the tension of the Troubles and was deprived of those later years when they could have enjoyed a more relaxed time together. One small consolation was the understanding and the reaction of the people of Derry city to John's deteriorating memory. There was no worry about his safety or dignity being compromised because all the people of the city became part of his 'carer' team. That outpouring of protection and love was perhaps the greatest tribute that was paid to him and his work.

I was driving home from Dublin when I heard Martin

McGuinness on the radio saying that he was resigning from the Stormont Executive, thus bringing down the coalition government between Sinn Féin and the DUP. To hear the exhaustion and the sickness in his voice was shocking. I went to visit him a few weeks later and a few weeks before his death. He certainly knew the pathology and the seriousness of his condition, but I don't know if he knew he was dying. His disappointment in Arlene Foster's refusal to stand down for a few weeks to allow the ramifications of the 'cash for ash' scandal to slightly dissipate and for the Executive to survive was palpable. He saw the Executive as one of his greatest achievements and the rejection of what he considered a pragmatic solution for both coalition parties annoyed him greatly. He and I had come together out of the exigencies of the time and the place. Both of us still lived in Derry, but the peace, ironically, resulted in less rather than more contact.

It would have been good to have had an opportunity for the four of us and others, such as Noel Gallagher, Michael Oatley and Fred, to have had time to chew the cud. To reminisce and fill in the gaps and the differing interpretations of events – not for an audience or for history, but for our own satisfaction. Life, death, sickness – events seldom allow that to happen, but even if those blockages were removed, the reality is that we men are too shy, or competitive, or unpractised in those conversations. The cud that we chew is seldom that personal. I have accused clerics of being proficient in this type of avoidance, but the truth is that men in general are adept at keeping themselves to themselves.

When I am asked or choose to write about the future of Northern Ireland, I am mostly positive, bordering on the optimistic. I see the politics of Ireland moving on a broad highway. There will be blockages, congestion and possibly a small number of diversions. But this unitary highway is the only road that has increasing traffic and a viable destination.

I was once part of a seminar with the late Fr Enda McDonagh, a very eminent theologian attached to Maynooth College, and the historian and journalist Ruth Dudley Edwards. In my input I said that the solution to the Troubles would be greatly influenced by demographics when the Catholic nationalist community came to outnumber the Protestant unionist community. I should acknowledge the insight of the late Frank Curran in this, who worked for years in the *Derry Journal* newspaper. He argued that demographic change would result less from Catholic birth rates than from Protestant death rates. He argued that the Protestant community was older, and the consequence of that was a decreasing population. However, at the seminar, my fellow panel members, especially McDonagh, thought my analysis was unworthy and crude. It is, of course, but it is an analysis and a reality that has come to the fore in the last few years. In the results of the last Northern Ireland census, the headline was that for the first time in a hundred years, Catholics outnumbered Protestants.

Demographic change is not the sole transformative cog in the wheel, but it is a pivotal one that opens the door to a lasting solution. It moves the focus onto the inevitability and the necessity of engagement between unionism and nationalism in working out and agreeing a long-term settlement. That is where we are stuck now. Unionism says that entering such a series of negotiations is an admission that the Union with Britain is coming to an end, while nationalism doesn't know how to entice or compel unionism into those negotiations. Ironically, the best argument on why a long-term settlement is needed was given by the politician who many would describe as the most trenchant unionist of all. Former First Minister Peter Robinson warned unionism that it needed a table, a forum, to discuss what he called a permanent solution. He said that political process had allowed devolution to function but that the process itself had eventually resulted in a feeling that everything is temporary, 'that the functioning of the Assembly will be repeatedly interrupted for negotiated pit-stops'. We are just out of one of those pit-stops now. He argued for permanence, saying, 'I am not talking of the shape of the new state that would emerge if there ever was a vote to exit the UK. I am alluding to the need to agree a process for negotiations, timescales and not only the means of reaching agreement on all the particulars but also who would be involved in negotiating such an agreement.' In the same statement he argued that there should be a fixed generational border poll which would provide clarity.

My analysis of his analysis is that he was telling unionism that it had no choice but to participate in a debate about the future, about the Union, about a shared island, about the political future of all nations in these islands. He was pointing out the need for a two-track approach – one to deal with everyday politics and one to deal with what he called a permanent solution and others called constitutional politics. He was observing that unless the constitutional issue was corralled onto its own track it would obstruct other politics from working. I agree.

Ironically, the unionist parties and the Irish government are on the same page in that both have turned a deaf ear to Robinson's advice. None of them promote a fundamental debate.

The 'Shared Island' unit established by the Irish government 'to enhance cooperation, connection and mutual understanding on the island and engage with all communities and traditions to build consensus around a shared future' is doing good work, but it has been accused of concentrating on the outer rings of the debate and staying away from the more contentious issues. It is also accused of showing little appetite for promoting any policy beyond making Northern Ireland work.

Nationalism is growing irritated with the continuing denial and blocking tactics being used by unionism. That is resulting in a growing emotional withdrawal from the already fragile belief that Northern Ireland can be made to work. Ironically, nationalism is more in tune and agreement with Robinson's thesis: that the debate is not happening with the seriousness and the clarity that is needed.

Because of the fragile institutions and the next election, which is always on the horizon, it is unlikely that any of the unionist parties will revisit Robinson's suggestion. It is also disappointing that since he expounded his thesis, he himself has not revisited or promoted it. Arlene Foster ignored it. Steve Aiken ignored it. Both have gone and been replaced. The DUP is being electorally sustained by the protocol that arises from the Brexit settlement, the resulting trading arrangement of which, the party argues, will signify a fracturing of the UK and an enhancement of commerce and trade within the island of Ireland. Perversely, its refusal to discuss a permanent solution ensures the growth of Sinn Féin in the North. Pitted against intransigence, Sinn Féin do not have to be politically astute or effective. They just have to be there.

In recent times, in very reduced political dialogue and writing,

I have been challenging the political party that attracts the most support from what is called the middle ground, the Alliance Party. I keep advising that the party needs to weigh the scales in support of seeking a permanent solution. So far, the response has been that its priority is to re-establish and sustain a reformed Northern Ireland Executive and achieve greater reconciliation between the two communities. The longer-term solution is not being ruled out but conversion to it is seen as a danger to the unity of the party. I would argue that the 'neutral' stance only sustains the present pit stops and delays the real and permanent agreement that is necessary and achievable.

The residue of the IRA, described as dissidents, still carry out the odd attack on the police and in their most notorious attack a few years back shot dead a young journalist, Lyra McKee. More recently they tried to murder a policeman in County Tyrone. Despite that, I detect a political debate taking place in their ranks between those who see the futility of their military 'sorties' and those who want to be a continuous stone in the shoe of all politics. There are indications coming out of sections of the security services that they want to keep their boot on the necks of these dissidents and have neither the desire nor the intention to offer them the penal agreements that were previously offered to both republican and loyalist paramilitaries. That is shortsighted.

So, while we continue to live with contested issues, with poor and often no devolved government and with the continuing presence of paramilitarism, I think the shadow of the Troubles hangs over us to some extent. The outline sketches for a shared island are being drawn up and while I might not live to see the implementation of whatever detailed plan ultimately emerges, I am convinced that it won't be that long until there is a coming together to agree and then to implement a political structure that fully includes both the Anglo and the Irish presence on this small island of Ireland.